Publisher
Entrepreneurial Learning Initiative, LLC

Director of Content Development
Gary Schoeniger

Senior Content Project Manager
Sam Kruse

Layout and Art Designer
Guillaume Muller-Greven

Content Contributors
Shash Woods, Joanie Weber

Executive Editor
Sam Kruse

Developmental Editor
Joanie Weber

Assistant Editor
Owen Schoeniger

TABLE OF CONTENTS

Welcome to the Ice House Entrepreneurship Program   7
Course Overview   7
Why Entrepreneurship?   7
Here's What You Can Expect   7
Before You Get Started   8
Here's How It Works   8
Accessing Your Class Online   8
Technical Support   10

Introduction Lesson   11
Overview   11
Lesson Objectives   11
Chalkboard Notes   12
Student-Generated Discussion   14
In-Class Discussion Notes   15
Reflection Assignment   17

Lesson 1: The Power to Choose   21
Overview   22
Lesson Objectives   22
Chalkboard Notes   23
Student-Generated Discussion   25
In-Class Discussion Notes   26
Application Assignment   28
Reflection Assignment   32

Lesson 2: Recognizing Opportunities   35
Overview   35
Lesson Objectives   35
Chalkboard Notes, Part 1   37
Student-Generated Discussion, Part 1   39
In-Class Discussion Notes, Part 1   40
Chalkboard Notes, Part 2   42
Student-Generated Discussion, Part 2   44
In-Class Discussion Notes, Part 2   45
Application Assignment   46
Reflection Assignment   51

The Ice House Opportunity Discovery Process   **54**

Problem-Based Learning   54
Experiential Learning   54
Kolb's Experiential Learning Cycle   55
Ice House Opportunity Discovery Canvas   56
Back of Canvas Analysis   59
Canvas in Action   60

Lesson 3: Ideas into Action   **71**

Overview   71
Lesson Objectives   72
Chalkboard Notes, Part 1   73
Student-Generated Discussion, Part 1   75
In-Class Discussion Notes, Part 1   76
Chalkboard Notes, Part 2   76
Student-Generated Discussion, Part 2   80
In-Class Discussion Notes, Part 2   81
Application Assignment   83
Peer Workshop Notes   88
Reflection Assignment   90

Lesson 4: Pursuit of Knowledge   **93**

Overview   93
Lesson Objectives   94
Chalkboard Notes, Part 1   95
Student-Generated Discussion, Part 1   97
In-Class Discussion Notes, Part 1   98
Chalkboard Notes, Part 2   100
Student-Generated Discussion, Part 2   102
In-Class Discussion Notes, Part 2   103
Application Assignment   105
Peer Workshop Notes   110
Reflection Assignment   112

Lesson 5: Creating Wealth — 115
Overview — 115
Lesson Objectives — 116
Chalkboard Notes, Part 1 — 117
Student-Generated Discussion, Part 1 — 119
'In-Class Discussion Notes, Part 1 — 120
Chalkboard Notes, Part 2 — 122
Student-Generated Discussion, Part 2 — 124
In-Class Discussion Notes, Part 2 — 125
Application Assignment — 128
Peer Workshop Notes — 132
Reflection Assignment — 134

Midterm Presentation — 137

Lesson 6: Building Your Brand — 138
Overview — 138
Lesson Objectives — 140
Chalkboard Notes, Part 1 — 141
Student-Generated Discussion, Part 1 — 143
In-Class Discussion Notes, Part 1 — 144
Chalkboard Notes, Part 2 — 146
Student-Generated Discussion, Part 2 — 148
In-Class Discussion Notes, Part 2 — 149
Application Assignment — 151
Peer Workshop Notes — 156
Reflection Assignment — 158

Lesson 7: Creating Community — 161
Overview — 161
Lesson Objectives — 162
Chalkboard Notes, Part 1 — 163
Student-Generated Discussion, Part 1 — 165
In-Class Discussion Notes, Part 1 — 166
Chalkboard Notes, Part 2 — 168
Student-Generated Discussion, Part 2 — 170
In-Class Discussion Notes, Part 2 — 171
Application Assignment — 173
Peer Workshop Notes — 178
Reflection Assignment — 180

Lesson 8: The Power of Persistence   **183**
Overview   183
Lesson Objectives   182
Chalkboard Notes, Part 1   185
Student-Generated Discussion, Part 1   187
In-Class Discussion Notes, Part 1   188
Chalkboard Notes, Part 2   190
Student-Generated Discussion, Part 2   192
In-Class Discussion Notes, Part 2   193
   Application Assignment   196
   Peer Workshop Notes   200
   Reflection Assignment   202

Final Presentation   **205**

Personal Vision Statement & Ice House Analysis   **207**

WELCOME TO THE ICE HOUSE ENTREPRENEURSHIP PROGRAM

As the creators of this course, we hope you find this class intellectually challenging, informative and engaging. Most of all, we hope this course will expose you to a new perspective; one that will reveal new opportunities, ignite your ambition and foster the attitudes, behaviors and skills that will empower you to succeed, both in school and in life.

Course Overview

This course is designed to inspire and engage students in the fundamental aspects of an entrepreneurial mindset and the unlimited opportunities it can provide. Sponsored by the Ewing Marion Kauffman Foundation, this program enables you to learn directly from the firsthand knowledge and experience drawn from a wide variety of successful "unlikely" entrepreneurs—ordinary people who transformed a simple idea into a sustainable success. Inspired by the life story of Pulitzer nominee Clifton Taulbert and the entrepreneurial influence of his Uncle Cleve, the Ice House Entrepreneurship Program draws on eight fundamental concepts that can empower anyone to succeed.

Why Entrepreneurship?

Entrepreneurship is a mindset that can empower ordinary people to accomplish extraordinary things. In today's rapidly changing world, it is a mindset that every student needs regardless of his or her chosen path.

Here's What You Can Expect:

This highly interactive program will enable you to learn directly from the first-hand experience of successful "unlikely" entrepreneurs. The overall objective is to expose you to the fundamental aspects of entrepreneurial thinking while immersing you in real-world entrepreneurial experiences that will enable you to develop entrepreneurial attitudes, behaviors and skills. After completing this course, you will be able to:

- Identify fundamental aspects of an entrepreneurial mindset.
- Identify and evaluate entrepreneurial opportunities.
- Develop entrepreneurial attitudes, behaviors and skills that can be applied across disciplines and as a means of personal empowerment and growth.
- Establish goals, identify resources and manage risks in unpredictable real-world circumstances.
- Identify and interact with local entrepreneurs and business owners within your own community who can provide valuable guidance and support.

Before You Get Started, there are a few things you should know:

Entrepreneurship is not a spectator sport—the more you put into the course, the more benefit you are likely to gain. The Ice House Entrepreneurship Program combines traditional classroom learning with real-world "out-of-the-building" experiences that will require you to solve problems in real-world circumstances where answers can be difficult to find and not always clear.

Throughout the program you will be encouraged to interact with potential "customers," as well as experienced entrepreneurs, small business owners and industry experts who can provide valuable insight, guidance and support. You will also be encouraged to share what you are learning with other students through in-class discussions, peer workshops and formal presentations.

Here's How It Works:

The Ice House Entrepreneurship Program is divided into eight individual lessons. Within each lesson there are six course elements.

1. **Companion text** *Who Owns the Ice House - Eight Life Lessons From An Unlikely Entrepreneur* by Clifton Taulbert and Gary Schoeniger. For each lesson, you will be required to read and discuss a corresponding chapter.

2. **Narrated Chalkboard Lessons** that combine basic bullet-point text and graphic illustrations with video interview segments featuring the firsthand knowledge and experience drawn from successful real-world entrepreneurs. True/False questions are randomly embedded as ungraded "checkpoints" between individual chapters. You must complete these questions before you can proceed to the next chapter of the lesson.

3. **Multiple Choice Assessments** are designed to ensure basic knowledge comprehension of the core concepts contained in the Chalkboard Lessons, as well as the Companion Text.

4. **Discussions** are designed to help stimulate peer-to-peer dialogue, synthesize knowledge and allow you to compare and contrast Ice House lessons with your own life experience and prior knowledge, in class or in online discussion forums.

5. **Application Assignments** are designed to immerse you in real-world entrepreneurial experiences that will enable you to develop entrepreneurial attitudes, behaviors and skills.

6. **Reflection Assignments** that provide an opportunity to reflect on the core Ice House concepts and how they can be applied in a way that will enable you to overcome obstacles and accomplish your goals.

See your facilitator for more detailed information regarding assignment due dates, grading requirements and other details. To get the most out of this course, we encourage you to:

1. Take notes as you view the narrated chalkboards to prepare for in-class discussions. Clicking on the "notes" tab in the upper left-hand corner will enable you to type and save your notes along the way. (The printer icon will enable you to print or save your notes as a separate file.)

2. Take your time. There is a lot of information to absorb. Take time to reflect on what you have learned and how it can be applied to your own life. Your individual reflections will form the basis of your personal vision statement at the end of the course.

3. Get out of your comfort zone. The course is designed to challenge and encourage you to learn in unpredictable real-world circumstances, which often expose unforeseen opportunities.

4. Share what you have learned with others by participating in the in-class discussions and peer workshops. Sharing new knowledge will also help retain more of what you learn.

5. See your instructor for additional details regarding project due dates, grading requirements and other course details.

Accessing Your Class Online:

You will receive a link to register for your class. This link will be contained in your course syllabus, your institution's learning management system, or in a registration email from your instructor. Please follow these steps to register:

1. Select link. Copy and paste link into web browser.
2. Fill in your personal information, create password, and submit form.
3. Select the course you are registering for.
4. Add course to cart & checkout with your discount code (contained in your student materials) or your credit card.

Note: Your course materials can be obtained from your institution's bookstore or from your instructor.

Technical Support:

For general questions about the Digital Chalk learning environment, click on the "help" button in the upper right hand corner of the learning environment. For technical support, contact support@digitalchalk.com.

If you encounter troubles with logging in to Digital Chalk, please attempt the following prior to contacting technical support:

1. Please remember that passwords are case sensitive.

2. If copying/pasting either your username or password into the form field, please be sure not to include extra spaces before or after, as this will result in an error.

3. Please select "I forgot my password" directly below the login button on Digital Chalk if you have misplaced your password.

For additional support and general questions about this course, contact **support@elientrepreneur.com**. And by all means, send us your feedback. Let us know what you got out of the course and what we can do to improve the learning experience.

INTRODUCTION LESSON

Overview

The introductory lesson offers a brief overview of the eight life lessons, an introduction to several of the Ice House Entrepreneurs, as well as a look beneath the surface to examine some of the most commonly held myths about what it really takes to succeed as an entrepreneur. We'll also introduce some basic concepts that are essential to understand.

1. What Will You Learn?
Chapter one provides a brief description of each of the eight life lessons.

2. Introduction to the Ice House Entrepreneurs
In chapter two, we'll introduce several of the Ice House Entrepreneurs who will describe in their own words the opportunities they found, the challenges they faced and the valuable lessons they learned along the way.

3. Unraveling the Mystery
Are entrepreneurs born with a unique ability or is entrepreneurship something that we can learn? In chapter three, we'll examine the myths and explore the reality of what it really takes to succeed as an entrepreneur.

4. Mindset Defined
What exactly is a mindset? The mindset may be the most important aspect of entrepreneurship, yet it may also be the most often overlooked and widely misunderstood. In this chapter, we'll define the term in a way that is actionable to an aspiring entrepreneur.

Lesson Objectives

The introductory lesson offers a brief overview of the eight life lessons and an introduction to several of the Ice House Entrepreneurs.

After completing the introduction lesson, participants will be able to:

- Identify the most commonly held myths about what it really takes to succeed as an entrepreneur.
- Define "mindset" in a way that is actionable to an aspiring entrepreneur.

Chalkboard Notes

Student-Generated Discussion

Once you have viewed this part of the Chalkboard Lesson, think about the core concepts contained in each lesson and create 1 or 2 questions or topics that you would like to discuss in class. Also, write a brief response to one of the following four prompts prior to the next in-class session.

1. Which concept from this Chalkboard Lesson was most intriguing to you? Why?
2. Which entrepreneur's comments most sparked your interest in this lesson? Why?
3. How do the concepts in this lesson apply to an entrepreneurial mindset?
4. How does this portion of Uncle Cleve's story resonate with your own life?

Submit your discussion questions and responses to your facilitator prior to the corresponding in-class session.

In-Class Discussion Notes

Reflection Assignment

Reflection Assignments are designed to encourage you to write reflectively about what you are learning and to explore ideas more deeply. These assignments also provide an opportunity to think about the future you want to create for yourself and how best to apply the knowledge you have gained in a way that will enable you to accomplish your goals.

Introduction: Describe the future you want to create. Before we can create the life we imagine, we must first imagine the life we want to create.

Assignment: Describe in as much detail as possible, the life you want to create for yourself.

Reflect on the following questions:

1. What matters most to you? What does success look like to you?
2. What are the most important things you want to make happen at school, in your life and in your career?
3. What are the greatest obstacles preventing you from accomplishing your goals?
4. How will you overcome these obstacles in order to accomplish your goals?
5. What skills do you need to succeed in school, in your career and in life?

Your reflection should be 1-2 pages and should demonstrate evidence of in-depth reflective thinking. Your viewpoints and interpretations should be insightful and supported by clear examples.

_____
_____
_____
_____
_____
_____
_____
_____
_____
_____
_____
_____
_____
_____
_____
_____

LESSON 1: THE POWER TO CHOOSE

Uncle Cleve's Message

The ability to choose the way we respond to our circumstances is perhaps the greatest power we have. It is a power that Clifton's uncle, Cleve Mormon, demonstrated throughout his life:

He had not a single advantage to claim over any of the others within his community and most were exposed to the same opportunities, yet many were simply blinded by their beliefs. He had no financial advantage—Uncle Cleve did not come from a wealthy family nor did he have access to venture capital investors or credit from a local bank. At that time, most banks would not even consider lending money to an African American. Uncle Cleve was an ordinary man whose only advantage was his mindset.

He had no intellectual or academic advantage—Uncle Cleve was a simple man of average intelligence who displayed no particular genius. Although he could read and write and he understood basic math, he had no specialized knowledge, technical training, or other skills to set him apart. His formal education likely did not extend beyond the sixth grade.

He had no political advantage—Uncle Cleve had no government contracts, inside knowledge, or special connections that enabled him to succeed. Uncle Cleve was an ordinary man whose only advantage was his mindset, a mindset that enabled him to choose a different life that allowed him to triumph over adversity as an entrepreneur. It was his mindset that awakened his curiosity and opened his eyes to the world around him. It was his mindset that enabled him to recognize opportunities that others could not see. It was his mindset that ignited within him a desire and determination that empowered him to triumph over adversity and succeed as an entrepreneur. Ultimately, it was his mindset that set his spirit free.

Overview

Life is not a lottery. The ability to choose the way we respond to our circumstances is fundamental to an entrepreneurial mindset. Using real-world examples, participants learn to recognize how choices, rather than circumstances, will ultimately shape our lives.

1. Influence
In chapter one we'll learn how our environment can influence our mindset and the decisions we make - decisions that may be holding us back.

2. React vs. Respond
Chapter two examines the difference between a reaction and a response. Students learn how entrepreneurs respond to their circumstances rather than react.

3. Locus of Control
Chapter three introduces the concept of an internal vs. external locus of control. In this chapter, we will examine both perspectives and discuss the outcomes of each.

4. Vision: The Power to Choose
In chapter four, we will learn how entrepreneurs use their imagination and vision to access the greatest power they have - the power to choose.

Lesson Objectives

Life is not a lottery. The ability to choose the way we respond to our circumstances is fundamental to an entrepreneurial mindset.

After completing Lesson 1, participants will be able to:

- Explain in what way we all have choices, regardless of our circumstances.
- Give examples of how environmental influences can shape a mindset.
- State the difference between a reaction and a response, citing real-life examples.
- Outline the sequence and timing between stimulus, reaction and response.
- List some benefits of responding vs. reacting citing real-life examples.
- Define internal and external locus of control.
- Compare the assumptions and outcomes of an external and an internal locus of control.
- Describe how the power to choose, having an internal locus of control, and creating a vision all contribute to an entrepreneurial mindset.
- Understand how concepts from this lesson can support college success.

Chalkboard Notes

Student-Generated Discussion

Once you have viewed this part of the Chalkboard Lesson, think about the core concepts contained in each lesson and create 1 or 2 questions or topics that you would like to discuss in class. Also, write a brief response to one of the following four prompts prior to the next in-class session.

1. Which concept from this Chalkboard Lesson was most intriguing to you? Why?
2. Which entrepreneur's comments most sparked your interest in this lesson? Why?
3. How do the concepts in this lesson apply to an entrepreneurial mindset?
4. How does this portion of Uncle Cleve's story resonate with your own life?

Submit your discussion questions and responses to your facilitator prior to the corresponding in-class session.

_____
_____
_____
_____
_____
_____
_____
_____
_____
_____
_____
_____
_____
_____
_____
_____
_____
_____
_____
_____
_____

In-Class Discussion Notes

Application Assignment

Life is not a lottery. The ability to choose the way we respond to our circumstances is fundamental to an entrepreneurial mindset.

Individual Assignment: Describe a successful person you know or someone in your community. This could be a small business owner, an executive, a self-employed professional, a professional services provider or a high-growth entrepreneur. Write a brief description of the person and how they managed to succeed.

Respond to the following questions:

1. What, if any, advantages did he or she have?
2. What challenges did he or she face?
3. What are the skills that enabled him or her to succeed professionally, academically, or personally?
4. How have his or her choices influenced his/her success?
5. How did his or her circumstances influence these choices?
6. What problem is he or she solving? Who is he or she solving that problem for?

Application Assignment

Application Assignment Rubric

Score	3	2	1	0
Criteria				
QUANTITY & ACCOUNTABILITY Central questions and directives in the assignment are addressed	☐ Selects a successful person to describe (or interview) ☐ Writes 250-300 word assignment ☐ Assignment is submitted on time	☐ Selects a successful person to describe ☐ Writes 250-300 word assignment ☐ Assignment is submitted on time	☐ Selects a successful person to describe ☐ Writes 250-300 word assignment	☐ Written assignment is not submitted
QUALITY & CONNECTION Information sources are relevant, and assignment demonstrates critical thinking skills	☐ Successful person is briefly described (or interviewed), and how they managed to succeed is plausibly outlined ☐ Assignment questions are all utilized to guide writing ☐ Answers to assignment questions are enriched by details and examples ☐ Successful person's story has been synthesized to describe a meaningful path to success ☐ Successful person described (or interviewed) is appropriate, and responses to questions clearly relate to an entrepreneurial mindset and the assignment objective.	☐ Successful person is briefly described, and how they managed to succeed is plausibly outlined ☐ Assignment questions are all utilized to guide writing ☐ Successful person described is appropriate, and responses to questions relate to an entrepreneurial mindset and the assignment objective.	☐ It is hard to understand the person's success story, because description is minimal and/or route to success is unclear ☐ Assignment question set is not followed or is incomplete	☐ Written assignment is not submitted

Reflection Assignment

Reflection assignments are designed to encourage you to write reflectively about what you are learning and to explore ideas more deeply. These assignments also provide an opportunity to think about the future you want to create for yourself and how to best apply the knowledge you have gained in a way that will enable you to accomplish your goals.

Life is not a lottery. The ability to choose the way we respond to our circumstances is fundamental to an entrepreneurial mindset.

Assignment: Reflect on the following questions:

1. What are the most important choices you have made in your life? How did your circumstances and mindset influence these choices?
2. What choices do you need to make to succeed in the future (personally, academically and professionally)? How will these choices determine your success?
3. What do you need to do more of? What do you need to do less of?
4. What do you need to start doing? What do you need to stop doing?

Your reflection should demonstrate evidence of in-depth reflective thinking. Your viewpoints and interpretations should be insightful and supported by clear examples.

_____
_____
_____
_____
_____
_____
_____
_____
_____
_____
_____
_____
_____
_____
_____
_____
_____
_____

LESSON 2: RECOGNIZING OPPORTUNITIES

Uncle Cleve's Message

Uncle Cleve was a problem solver. He understood that problems were opportunities and that if he could identify problems and find solutions for other people, he would prosper as well. He did not set out simply to make money for himself. He paid attention to the world around him, staying attuned to problems and issues that others complained about—especially the issues that he could address or improve. He was curious and his mind was constantly engaged, perpetually searching for solutions to the problems of others within his community. Everyone in Glen Allan needed ice. Uncle Cleve's solutions were not complex; much like delivering coal or wood or fixing cars, these issues did not involve revolutionary new technology or highly specialized knowledge. They did not require large sums of money or access to power and privilege. They were simple solutions to commonplace problems, solutions that were propelled by common sense, solutions rooted in reliability, good service—and a willingness to work long hours and take small risks.

Overview

Problems are often opportunities in disguise. Entrepreneurs are problem solvers and the secret to their success lies in their ability to identify problems and find solutions. In this lesson, we will learn how to identify problems and use knowledge and experience to find solutions.

1. In Search of Opportunity
In chapter one, we'll examine the importance of balancing the "right" idea with our abilities as an entrepreneur.

2. Problems are Opportunities
In chapter two, we'll examine some of the fundamental concepts and the underlying assumptions that enable entrepreneurs to identify opportunities regardless of their circumstances.

3. Simple Solutions
In chapter three, we'll see how entrepreneurs with limited resources transform simple solutions into successful new ventures.

4. Opportunistic Adaptation

In chapter four, we'll describe the process of opportunistic adaptation. We'll see how entrepreneurs often uncover unforeseen opportunities through the process of interaction and observation, experimentation and adaptation.

5. Prior Work Experience

In chapter five, we'll discuss where to look for opportunities. While some set out in search of a big idea, we'll see how entrepreneurs learn to identify opportunities in their own backyard.

6. Enthusiastic and Somewhat Inexperienced

Contrary to popular belief, we do not need to be an "expert" to become an entrepreneur. In chapter six, we'll see how successful entrepreneurs overcome their lack of experience to succeed.

7. Inventor as Entrepreneur

In chapter seven, we'll learn directly from a very successful inventor and entrepreneur who will describe the process of identifying problems and finding solutions.

Lesson Objectives

Problems are often opportunities in disguise. Entrepreneurs are problem solvers and the secret to their success lies in their ability to identify and solve problems regardless of what they have to work with or where they start.

After completing Lesson 2, participants will be able to:

- Explain how entrepreneurs identify problems as potential opportunities.
- Explain how problem-solving ability is a key aspect of an entrepreneurial mindset.
- Describe a business that provides a simple, reliable solution to an everyday problem.
- Define the concept of opportunistic adaptation.
- Identify five fatal assumptions that can hinder an entrepreneurial endeavor.
- Understand how concepts from this lesson can support college success.

Chalkboard Notes, Part 1

37

Student-Generated Discussion, Part 1

Once you have viewed this part of the Chalkboard Lesson, think about the core concepts contained in each lesson and create 1 or 2 questions or topics that you would like to discuss in class. Also, write a brief response to one of the following four prompts prior to the next in-class session.

1. Which concept from this Chalkboard Lesson was most intriguing to you? Why?
2. Which entrepreneur's comments most sparked your interest in this lesson? Why?
3. How do the concepts in this lesson apply to an entrepreneurial mindset?
4. How does this portion of Uncle Cleve's story resonate with your own life?

Submit your discussion questions and responses to your facilitator prior to the corresponding in-class session.

_____
_____
_____
_____
_____
_____
_____
_____
_____
_____
_____
_____
_____
_____
_____
_____
_____
_____
_____
_____
_____
_____

In-Class Discussion Notes, Part 1

41

Chalkboard Notes, Part 2

Student-Generated Discussion, Part 2

Once you have viewed this part of the Chalkboard Lesson, think about the core concepts contained in each lesson and create 1 or 2 questions or topics that you would like to discuss in class. Also, write a brief response to one of the following four prompts prior to the next in-class session.

1. Which concept from this Chalkboard Lesson was most intriguing to you? Why?
2. Which entrepreneur's comments most sparked your interest in this lesson? Why?
3. How do the concepts in this lesson apply to an entrepreneurial mindset?
4. How does this portion of Uncle Cleve's story resonate with your own life?

Submit your discussion questions and responses to your facilitator prior to the corresponding in-class session.

_____

_____

_____

_____

_____

_____

_____

_____

_____

_____

_____

_____

_____

_____

_____

_____

_____

_____

_____

_____

_____

_____

_____

_____

In-Class Discussion Notes, Part 2

Application Assignment

Problems are often opportunities in disguise. Entrepreneurs are problem solvers. The secret to their success lies in their ability to identify and solve problems regardless of what they have to work with or where they start.

Individual Assignment: Identify at least 3 problems, frustrations, or unmet needs that you have encountered in your personal life, through a work experience or in school. For each problem you identify, answer the following questions.

1. Describe the problem, frustration, or unmet need.
2. Why is the solution to this problem important to you?
3. Do other people have this problem?
4. How are they currently solving the problem?
5. How might you offer a better solution?

Discuss each of the problems with friends, family members and others who may also have an interest in solving the problem. Describe which of the problems is most important to you and why? Be prepared to discuss these problems in class.

Application Assignment

_____

_____

_____

_____

_____

_____

_____

_____

_____

_____

_____

_____

_____

_____

_____

_____

_____

_____

_____

_____

_____

_____

_____

_____

_____

_____

_____

_____

_____

_____

_____

_____

_____

_____

_____

_____

_____

_____

Application Assignment Rubric

Score	3	2	1	0
Criteria				
QUANTITY & ACCOUNTABILITY Central questions and directives in the assignment are addressed	□ Three or more problems are identified □ Writes 250-300 word assignment □ Assignment is submitted on time	□ At least 3 problems are identified □ Writes 250-300 word assignment □ Assignment is submitted on time	□ 1 – 3 problems are identified □ Writes 250-300 word assignment	□ Written assignment is not submitted
QUALITY & CONNECTION Information sources are relevant, and assignment demonstrates critical thinking skills	□ Identified problems come from actual experiences in personal life, work, or school □ Problems are relevant to community (not just student) and solution could realistically be found □ Complete question set is addressed for each problem □ Writing shows evidence of consulting friends, family, and/or community members □ Participation in class discussion shows thoughtful consideration of the importance of problems selected	□ Identified problems come from actual experiences in personal life, work, or school. □ Problems are relevant to community (not just student) and solution could realistically be found □ Majority of questions are addressed for each problem □ Discusses selected problems in class	□ Problems identified may be realistic, but discussion with others has not been used to develop them more deeply □ Question set is not used, or is used incompletely	□ Written assignment is not submitted

Reflection Assignment

Reflection assignments are designed to encourage you to write reflectively about what you are learning and to explore ideas more deeply. These assignments also provide an opportunity to think about the future you want to create for yourself and how best to apply the knowledge you have gained in a way that will enable you to accomplish your goals.

Problems are often opportunities in disguise. Entrepreneurs are problem solvers and the secret to their success lies in their ability to identify problems and find solutions.

Assignment: Reflect on the following questions:

1. When you encounter a problem, do you tend to think about possible solutions or do you tend to focus only on the problem?
2. How do you need to approach problems you encounter in life, at work and at school in the future?
3. What stands out to you, feels new to you, excites you, or challenges you from this lesson?

Your reflection should demonstrate evidence of in-depth reflective thinking. Your viewpoints and interpretations should be insightful and supported by clear examples.

_____

_____

_____

_____

_____

_____

_____

_____

_____

_____

_____

_____

_____

_____

_____

_____

_____

_____
_____
_____
_____
_____
_____
_____
_____
_____
_____
_____
_____
_____
_____
_____
_____
_____
_____
_____
_____
_____
_____
_____
_____
_____
_____
_____
_____
_____
_____
_____
_____
_____
_____

THE ICE HOUSE OPPORTUNITY DISCOVERY PROCESS

Now that you have reached the end of lesson 2, we will introduce the Opportunity Discovery Canvas, a tool that will guide you through the Opportunity Discovery Process. The discovery process is iterative and problem-based, and lies at the core of understanding and applying an entrepreneurial mindset. It is an experiential learning process designed to help you develop entrepreneurial attitudes, behaviors and skills. You will use the canvas as a tool to go "out-of-the-building" and search for problem-solving opportunities throughout the remaining group application assignments.

Problem-Based Learning

Problem-based learning is a fundamental aspect of the Opportunity Discovery Process. It is a process in which you will learn from complex and realistic problem solving situations. Problem-based learning will help develop critical thinking and effective problem solving skills. Problem-based learning also encourages collaboration, intrinsic motivation and self-directed learning.

Experiential Learning

The Opportunity Discovery Process is also an experiential learning process, one that enables you to learn from experience. It is among the most powerful tools available to help develop entrepreneurial attitudes, behaviors and skills. Drawing from David Kolb's experiential learning model, the Opportunity Discovery Process immerses you in an iterative, four stage process:

1. In the "concrete experience" stage, you become aware of a problem or unmet need.

2. This awareness forms the basis for "observation and reflection" where you will have the opportunity to observe the problem and consider what is working or failing.

3. You will then think about ways to solve the problem or improve an existing solution, a process known as "abstract conceptualization".

4. Facilitators will then encourage you to test your solutions through "active experimentation" and interaction with those who may also experience the problem.

Experiential learning requires you to actively engage in the experience, and then to reflect on your experiences so as to understand, analyze and apply new knowledge. It is an iterative, experimental process that lies at the core of an entrepreneur's ability to identify, evaluate and solve problems within real-world, ambiguous circumstances.

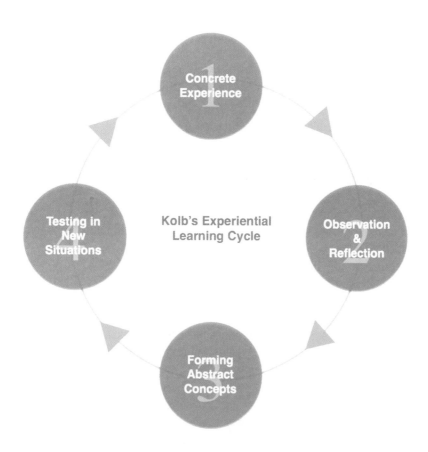

The Ice House Opportunity Discovery Canvas

The Ice House Opportunity Discovery Canvas is a tool designed to guide you through the Opportunity Discovery Process. Drawing on the work of Alexander Osterwalder's Business Model Canvas, the Opportunity Discovery Canvas encourages you to think critically as you learn to identify and solve problems within uncertain circumstances.

The Opportunity Discovery Canvas is divided into three primary sections designed to guide you through the three distinct phases of the Opportunity Discovery Process.

Section one encourages you to focus on the problem you intend to solve. Section two encourages you to consider possible solutions. Section three encourages you to think about how you might connect with others who may have the problem you intend to solve.

At the end of lesson 2, you will be asked to share your problem-solving ideas with the class, and then form into small canvas groups of 2 to 4 people based on these ideas. In your new canvas groups, you should document your assumptions or "best guesses" by addressing the questions within each of the canvas boxes. Once you have documented your assumptions in the appropriate boxes, you will get out-of-the-building to test your assumptions by interviewing potential customers and other stakeholders.

> **For example,** after learning of a robbery at a local bank, featured Ice House Entrepreneur David Petite envisioned a unique security device for ATM machines. As part of his discovery process, he identified bank managers as potential customers that he could interview as a way to determine the viability of his idea.
>
> He also identified law enforcement officials as potential stakeholders who could help validate the viability of his idea. Through the process of interviewing potential customers and stakeholders, he gained the confidence to develop a prototype of his concept.

In addition to interviewing potential customers and stakeholders, you should also seek additional knowledge through interaction with experienced entrepreneurs and subject matter experts, as well as traditional academic research methods.

Drawing on an experiential learning model, the Opportunity Discovery Process requires you to continuously analyze and revise your canvas assumptions based on what you are learning through the Opportunity Discovery Process. Your canvas will constantly change during the search for a problem-solution-connection, as your knowledge expands and your ideas continuously evolve. Each version of the canvas will build upon previous iterations.

Ice House Opportunity Discovery Canvas

1. Describe the problem you want to solve.

- How did you encounter this problem or unmet need?
- Do other people have this problem?
- Why is this problem worth solving?

2. Describe the type of people who have this problem.

- Describe the people that are most likely to have this problem?
- Think about age range, gender, areas of interest, profession, etc.
- Which of these potential "customers" can you most easily connect with?

3. How are they currently solving the problem?

- Describe other solutions that are currently available?
- Why is the current solution inadequate?
- How important is this problem?

4. Describe your proposed solution.

- What is the single most important feature of your solution?
- What is the most effective way to demonstrate your idea?
- How will you know if others are interested in your solution?

5. How will your solution be different?

- How does your idea better than existing solutions?
- Describe the key differences?
- How will you know if others value this improvement?

6. Will people pay for your solution?

- Will people be willing to pay for your solution?
- How often will they need your solution?
- How will you know that your solution is valuable to others?

7. How will potential customers know about your solution?

- How can you find more people who may be interested in your solution?
- What methods of communication will you use to reach them?
- What message do you intend to convey?

8. How will potential customers purchase your solution?

- How can you make it easy for your customers to purchase your solution?
- For example, through a retail store, online, door-to-door sales, etc.
- How are they currently accessing a solution?

9. Why will potential customers purchase your solution?

- How will your customers know they can rely on you?
- How will you communicate this message explicitly?
- Why is this problem worth solving?

PROBLEM · SOLUTION · CONNECTION

Sample Canvas

NOTES

1. What have you learned and how has your idea changed in the most recent version of your canvas?
    Which of your assumptions were accurate and which of them have changed?

    _____

    _____

    _____

    _____

    _____

    _____

    _____

2. What are your next action steps? Who do you still need to talk to and what knowledge gaps still
    need to be filled? How can you test your assumptions in the real world with limited time, money,
    and resources?

    _____

    _____

    _____

    _____

    _____

    _____

    _____

3. Additional Analysis

    _____

    _____

    _____

    _____

    _____

    _____

    _____

    _____

    _____

    _____

Sample Notes

Back of Canvas Analysis

The back side of each Opportunity Discovery Canvas includes a "Notes" section designed for you to analyze and reflect on what you are learning as you complete each iteration of your canvas. The back of the canvas includes the following questions:

- What have you learned and how has your idea changed in the most recent version of your canvas?

- Which of your assumptions were accurate and which of them have changed?

- What are your next action steps?

- Who do you still need to talk to and what knowledge gaps still need to be filled?

- How can you test your assumptions in the real world with limited time, money, and resources?

When does the Opportunity Discovery Process end?

Generally the process ends in one of two ways: Your group decides it no longer wants to pursue a particular solution and you begin to search for other problems to solve; or your group has validated its concept and people are beginning to pay for your solution. The overall objective is to help you develop effective problem-solving skills.

Canvas in Action

The following is a detailed explanation of each phase of the Opportunity Discovery Process. This explanation includes example canvases that illustrate several iterations of the entrepreneurial process for Jason Campbell, one of the Ice House Entrepreneurs.

Phase 1: Understanding the Problem

The first row of boxes (1 through 3) encourage you to focus on the problem you intend to solve or the unmet need you intend to fill. These initial questions are designed to gain an "outside-in" perspective that enables you to understand the problem through the eyes of potential customers or stakeholders before prescribing a potential solution. While you may already have a potential solution in mind, the emphasis here should be on accurately understanding the problem.

In addition to the primary question within each box, additional questions or suggestions are included to help guide the inquiry and discovery process. These secondary questions are intended merely as a guide to help you through the discovery process.

Box 1: Describe the problem you want to solve.

- How did you encounter this problem or unmet need?
- Do other people have this problem?
- Why is this problem worth solving?

Box 2: Describe the type of people who have this problem.

- Describe the people that are most likely to have this problem.
- Think about age range, gender, areas of interest, profession, etc.
- Which of these potential "customers" can you most easily connect with?

Box 3: How are they currently solving the problem?

- Describe other solutions that are currently available.
- Why is the current solution inadequate?
- How important is this problem?

Ice House Opportunity Discovery Canvas

1. Describe the problem you want to solve.	2. Describe the type of people who have this problem.	3. How are they currently solving the problem?
Home-builders have difficulty maintaining clean, organized construction sites	Smaller construction Companies and independent Contractor	Not sure? Maybe owners are doing it themselves?

PROBLEM

4. Describe your proposed solution.	5. How will your solution be different?	6. Will people pay for your solution?

SOLUTION

7. How will potential customers know about your solution?	8. How will potential customers purchase your solution?	9. Why will potential customers purchase your solution?

CONNECTION

Example Canvas 1

NOTES

1. What have you learned and how has your idea changed in the most recent version of your canvas? Which of your assumptions were accurate and which of them have changed?

   Not yet applicable - have not been out of building yet.

2. What are your next action steps? Who do you still need to talk to and what knowledge gaps still need to be filled? How can you test your assumptions in the real world with limited time, money, and resources?

   Speak to 5 building contractors to discuss problem, inquire about possible solutions.

   Questions: how often do sites need to be cleaned? Does cleaning require special equipment like garbage dumpsters? Would I have to dispose of waste myself? Talk to waste removal companies.

3. Additional Analysis

   Identify areas where there are construction activities. Identify people we know who may own small construction companies.

   Identify people who may work in construction industry

   Identify people who may work in related industries like carpentry, masonry work, excavation, plumbing, electricians, bankers (who work with construction loans).

Example Notes 1

Phase 2: Solution

The second row of boxes (4 through 6) are solution-oriented questions that encourage you to think about potential solutions, as well as the viability of your proposed solutions. You should test your ideas by interviewing potential customers and other stakeholders who may have an interest in solving the problem at hand. In many (if not most) cases, the original idea is likely to be flawed. Yet through this interactive discovery process unforeseen obstacles, as well as unexpected opportunities, can be found.

Box 4: Describe your proposed solution.

- What is the single most important feature of your solution?
- What is the most effective way to demonstrate your idea?
- How will you know if others are interested in your solution?

Box 5: How will your solution be different?

- Why is your idea better than existing solutions?
- Describe the key differences.
- How will you know if others value this improvement?

Box 6: Will people pay for your solution?

- Will people be willing to pay for your solution?
- How often will they need your solution?
- How will you know that your solution is valuable to others?

# Ice House Opportunity Discovery Canvas

1. Describe the problem you want to solve.	2. Describe the type of people who have this problem.	3. How are they currently solving the problem?
Home-builders have difficulty maintaining clean, organized construction sites	Smaller construction Companies and independent Contractors. Very small – one-man – contracting Companies not interested. They do it themselves	~~Not sure? Maybe owners are doing it themselves?~~ Small contractors doing it themselves.

PROBLEM

4. Describe your proposed solution.	5. How will your solution be different?	6. Will people pay for your solution?
Reliable service on-demand site cleaning services	Reliable on-demand site cleaning services	Yes – $20 per hour rate

SOLUTION

7. How will potential customers know about your solution?	8. How will potential customers purchase your solution?	9. Why will potential customers purchase your solution?

CONNECTION

Example Canvas 2

NOTES

1. What have you learned and how has your idea changed in the most recent version of your canvas? Which of your assumptions were accurate and which of them have changed?

   Yes - construction site cleaning seems to a real problem. Owners of construction companies were more helpful/open than I expected. Small companies don't have the staff, or much time to find outside help for site cleaning.

   Construction sites almost always have garbage dumpsters on them, so this shouldn't be a problem. Sometimes I may have to arrange dumpster drop off/pick up (easy to do).

2. What are your next action steps? Who do you still need to talk to and what knowledge gaps still need to be filled? How can you test your assumptions in the real world with limited time, money, and resources?

   Need to determine what specific tools I need (like vacuums, brooms, buckets and protective clothing, etc). Contact trash removal company for prices. Do I need permits, if so who do I talk to? City building inspectors? Construction sites have heavy equipment and expensive materials, do I need insurance? Confirm with contractors, then find business insurance companies and determine costs.

3. Additional Analysis

   Identify who in group will explore tools, permits, insurance, pricing etc.

   Since contractors were so open and willing to talk to me, I think there's a fair amount of interest in this service. The work is straightforward & satisfying, and valuable enough to the contractors for a very reasonable $20 hourly rate. This idea is definitely worth pursuing.

   Will contractors be willing to pay an hourly rate? Won't they worry about being overbilled, or people taking their time to perform the work?

Example Notes 2

Phase 3: Problem-Solution-Connection

Once a problem-solution fit has been confirmed, the third row of boxes (7 through 9) encourages you to think about broadening your reach by connecting with more people who may have the problem you are trying to solve.

While you are asked to consider these connection questions as part of the group application assignment in lesson 6, you should still continuously test your ideas and confirm a problem-solution fit (boxes 1 through 6) before investing too much time and effort attempting to connect with a broader audience.

Box 7: How will potential customers know about your solution?

- How can you find more people who may be interested in your solution?
- What methods of communication will you use to reach them?
- What message do you intend to convey?

Box 8: How will potential customers purchase your solution?

- How can you make it easy for your customers to purchase your solution?
- For example, through a retail store, online, door-to-door sales, etc.
- How are they currently accessing a solution?

Box 9: Why will potential customers purchase your solution?

- How will your customers know they can rely on you?
- How will you communicate this message explicitly?
- How will you communicate this message implicitly?

Ice House Opportunity Discovery Canvas

1. Describe the problem you want to solve.	2. Describe the type of people who have this problem.	3. How are they currently solving the problem?
Home-builders have difficulty maintaining clean, organized construction sites	Smaller construction Companies and independent Contractors Very small - one-man - contracting Companies not interested. They do it themselves	Small contractors doing it themselves.

PROBLEM

4. Describe your proposed solution.	5. How will your solution be different?	6. Will people pay for your solution?
Reliable service on-demand site cleaning services	Reliable on-demand site cleaning services	~~Yes - $20 per hour rate~~ Customers prefer to pay by the job rather than hourly rate

SOLUTION

7. How will potential customers know about your solution?	8. How will potential customers purchase your solution?	9. Why will potential customers purchase your solution?
Simple one-page flyers, word of mouth	Call on-demand short notice.	Reliability is the key. Customers must know that we will complete jobs/projects on time - no excuses.

CONNECTION

Example Canvas 3

NOTES

1. What have you learned and how has your idea changed in the most recent version of your canvas? Which of your assumptions were accurate and which of them have changed?

Customers prefer to pay by the project rather than by the hour. This makes sense because it's less risky for them (they don't have to worry about being overbilled, etc).

But this means we have to be good at estimating how much time jobs will take, so we don't end up working for pennies.

Reliability is definitely important because contractors have very tight scheduling for the different phases of construction projects, showing the property to potential customers, etc.

2. What are your next action steps? Who do you still need to talk to and what knowledge gaps still need to be filled? How can you test your assumptions in the real world with limited time, money, and resources?

Need to determine how to connect with more customers, as well as identifying other related services we can offer.

Need to determine pricing, document time spent to complete projects.

Need to plan for growth by recruiting more team members. Follow up with other construction related companies to offer related services.

Talk to lawyer for basic legal advice.

3. Additional Analysis

May be able to set a project price - we manage the construction site cleaning throughout the project without needing to be prompted by contractor (need to remove this area of concern).

Need to improve messaging on flyer to let potential customers know we offer other services as well (experiment with different service offerings, see what people call back about). Need to figure out how to get other related companies to promote/talk about our services.

Example Notes 3

LESSON 3: IDEAS INTO ACTION

Uncle Cleve's Message

Uncle Cleve was a man of action. He was always in motion and his mind was always fully engaged. Once he had identified an opportunity and gathered the information he needed, he set his plan into motion. He was not one to make excuses and he was not afraid to try something new. Although he had no formal education, he was not afraid to learn. He acted on his ideas and gave little credence to what others thought of him. He focused his precious time and energy on things he could change and work was not his enemy. Rather than approaching work as an unpleasant experience, it was something he took pride in; something he enjoyed. In spite of the circumstances that surrounded him and the limitations that were beyond his control, he chose to focus on those things that he could change. He understood the power of his actions and fully embraced the qualities of the entrepreneurial mindset.

Overview

Think big. Start small. Act fast. Entrepreneurs are action oriented and they tend to focus their time and energy on things they can change rather than things they cannot. Using case studies, participants learn how entrepreneurs overcome self-imposed limitations and put their ideas into action.

1. Barriers to Entry
In chapter one, we'll define the barriers that prevent us from acting on our ideas.

2. Lack of Money
In chapter two, we'll discuss the lack of money as an obstacle that can be overcome.

3. Bootstrapping
In chapter three, we'll explore the concept of bootstrapping. We'll learn how entrepreneurs manage to make it work with what they've got by "bootstrapping" their way into business.

4. Proof of Concept
In chapter four, we will discuss the importance of "proving your concept". We'll see how entrepreneurs with limited resources "prove their concepts" with real customers.

5. Lack of Time
In chapter five, we'll explore the lack of time as an obstacle that entrepreneurs learn to overcome.

6. Lack of Experience

In chapter six, we'll discuss the lack of experience as a barrier and how every entrepreneur must learn to overcome it.

7. Fear

In chapter seven, we'll identify fear and self-doubt as a barrier that many entrepreneurs learn to overcome.

8. Reinventing Work

In chapter eight, we'll examine the motivation and the perspective that drives entrepreneurs to succeed.

Lesson Objectives

Think big. Start small. Act fast. Entrepreneurs are action oriented and they tend to focus their time and energy on things they can change rather than things they cannot.

After completing Lesson 3, participants will be able to:

- ▪ Explain how entrepreneurs identify problems as potential opportunities.
- ▪ Define "barriers to entry" and list several examples that can inhibit acting on ideas.
- ▪ Evaluate the relationship between a lack of money and the ability to start a business.
- ▪ Define "bootstrapping" as a solution for those who may not have access to investment.
- ▪ Define "proof of concept" as a way to evaluate a potential opportunity.
- ▪ Explain the customer's role in bootstrapping and in validating a solution.
- ▪ Apply the framework of locus of control to overcoming the obstacle of lack of time.
- ▪ Describe how knowledge combined with effort can overcome the lack of experience.
- ▪ Compare and contrast a fixed vs. a growth mindset.
- ▪ Define extrinsic motivation and intrinsic motivation.
- ▪ Summarize the value of putting ideas into action.
- ▪ Understand how concepts from this lesson can support college success.

Chalkboard Notes, Part 1

Student-Generated Discussion, Part 1

Once you have viewed this part of the Chalkboard Lesson, think about the core concepts contained in each lesson and create 1 or 2 questions or topics that you would like to discuss in class. Also, write a brief response to one of the following four prompts prior to the next in-class session.

1. Which concept from this Chalkboard Lesson was most intriguing to you? Why?
2. Which entrepreneur's comments most sparked your interest in this lesson? Why?
3. How do the concepts in this lesson apply to an entrepreneurial mindset?
4. How does this portion of Uncle Cleve's story resonate with your own life?

Submit your discussion questions and responses to your facilitator prior to the corresponding in-class session.

_____
_____
_____
_____
_____
_____
_____
_____
_____
_____
_____
_____
_____
_____
_____
_____
_____
_____
_____
_____
_____
_____
_____
_____

In-Class Discussion Notes, Part 1

Chalkboard Notes, Part 2

Student-Generated Discussion, Part 2

Once you have viewed this part of the Chalkboard Lesson, think about the core concepts contained in each lesson and create 1 or 2 questions or topics that you would like to discuss in class. Also, write a brief response to one of the following four prompts prior to the next in-class session.

1. Which concept from this Chalkboard Lesson was most intriguing to you? Why?
2. Which entrepreneur's comments most sparked your interest in this lesson? Why?
3. How do the concepts in this lesson apply to an entrepreneurial mindset?
4. How does this portion of Uncle Cleve's story resonate with your own life?

Submit your discussion questions and responses to your facilitator prior to the corresponding in-class session.

In-Class Discussion Notes, Part 2

81

Application Assignment

Now it's time to get out of the building and "hit the bricks" to begin testing your ideas in the real world. In this initial phase of the Opportunity Discovery Process, the goal is to test your assumptions by interviewing a variety of potential "customers" and other stakeholders who may also have an interest in the problem that you are trying to solve.

Group Assignment: Review the initial assumptions you documented in the Opportunity Discovery Canvas. Identify potential customers and other stakeholders who may have an interest in solving the problem at hand - the people you described in box 2 of your canvas. Using the questions in canvas boxes 1 through 3 as your guide, each team member should interview a minimum of 5 potential customers. The interviews should be conducted in a face-to-face format.

Action Steps:

- Discuss the problem you intend to solve. Do they share your frustration? Did they mention other problems that may be worth solving?
- Evaluate whether the problem is important to them. What evidence do you have?
- How are they currently solving the problem?
- Optional: If you have a proposed solution, ask if your solution makes sense.

Group Directive: As a group, review your initial assumptions and revise boxes 1 through 3 of your Opportunity Discovery Canvas based on what you have learned from these initial interviews.

Note: While this assignment will focus primarily on the problem, those who already have a potential solution may complete additional boxes within the Opportunity Discovery Canvas.

Back of the Canvas Analysis: Complete the Notes section on the back side of the canvas worksheet (approximately 100-150 words). In the "Additional Analysis" section of your Notes, consider the following questions:

- How would you rate your customers' level of interest in the problem or solution? (Strongly interested, somewhat interested, not interested, unclear, etc.)
- Are you confident that this problem is worth solving or do adjustments need to be made?
- What, if anything, surprised you the most from this interview experience?

Ice House Opportunity Discovery Canvas

1. Describe the problem you want to solve.	2. Describe the type of people who have this problem.	3. How are they currently solving the problem?

PROBLEM

4. Describe your proposed solution.	5. How will your solution be different?	6. Will people pay for your solution?

SOLUTION

7. How will potential customers know about your solution?	8. How will potential customers purchase your solution?	9. Why will potential customers purchase your solution?

CONNECTION

NOTES

1. What have you learned and how has your idea changed in the most recent version of your canvas? Which of your assumptions were accurate and which of them have changed?

    _____
    _____
    _____
    _____
    _____
    _____
    _____

2. What are your next action steps? Who do you still need to talk to and what knowledge gaps still need to be filled? How can you test your assumptions in the real world with limited time, money, and resources?

    _____
    _____
    _____
    _____
    _____
    _____
    _____

3. Additional Analysis

    _____
    _____
    _____
    _____
    _____
    _____
    _____
    _____
    _____
    _____
    _____

Application Assignment Rubric

Score → Criteria ↓	3	2	1	0
QUANTITY & ACCOUNTABILITY Central questions and directives in the assignment are addressed	☐ Each team member conducts face-to-face interviews with at least 5 potential customers (INDIVIDUAL) ☐ Boxes 1 – 3 of the canvas are revised based on insights from the interviews ☐ Notes section on the back side of the canvas worksheet is completed (100-150 words) ☐ Additional Analysis section of Notes is completed ☐ Assignment is submitted on time	☐ Each team member interviews at least 5 potential customers (INDIVIDUAL) ☐ Boxes 1 – 3 of the canvas are revised based on insights from the interviews ☐ Notes section on the back side of the canvas is completed (100-150 words) ☐ Assignment is submitted on time	☐ Some team members do not conduct at least 5 interviews (INDIVIDUAL) ☐ Boxes 1 – 3 of the canvas are revised based on insights from the interviews ☐ Notes section on the back side of the canvas is completed	☐ Individuals do not conduct interviews ☐ Canvas is not revised
QUALITY & CONNECTION Information sources are relevant, and assignment demonstrates critical thinking skills	☐ Potential customers interviewed clearly have a stake in the Canvas problem (INDIVIDUAL) ☐ Complete question set is addressed during interviews (INDIVIDUAL) ☐ Canvas revisions are justified and explained with evidence from interviews ☐ Potential solution created and canvas boxes 4 - 6 are also filled in (Optional). ☐ Notes section directly address changes in the most recent canvas iteration and adjustments to previous assumptions ☐ Next action steps make sense to fill gaps in knowledge and continue discovery process ☐ Additional Analysis in Notes addresses assignment questions ☐ Analysis judgments are defended with interview evidence	☐ Potential customers interviewed clearly have a stake in the canvas problem (INDIVIDUAL) ☐ Interview questions are drawn from suggested question set (INDIVIDUAL) ☐ Canvas revisions are justified and explained with evidence from interviews ☐ Notes section directly address changes in the most recent canvas iteration ☐ Action steps make sense to fill gaps in knowledge and further discovery ☐ Next action steps are concrete and timely ☐ Analysis judgments are defended with interview evidence	☐ The majority of potential customers interviewed have a stake in the canvas problem or solution posed (INDIVIDUAL) ☐ Interview questions are drawn from suggested question set (INDIVIDUAL) ☐ Canvas revisions are made, but evidence to support revisions may be limited, or not convincingly applied ☐ New and/or old ideas may be written in Notes, but are not directly compared ☐ Next action steps are minimal or not well thought through	☐ Individuals do not conduct interviews ☐ Canvas is not revised

Peer Workshop Notes

_____
_____
_____
_____
_____
_____
_____
_____
_____
_____
_____
_____
_____
_____
_____
_____
_____
_____
_____
_____
_____
_____
_____
_____
_____
_____
_____
_____
_____
_____
_____
_____
_____

Reflection Assignment

Reflection assignments are designed to encourage you to write reflectively about what you are learning and to explore ideas more deeply. These assignments also provide an opportunity to think about the future you want to create for yourself and how best to apply the knowledge you have gained in a way that will enable you to accomplish your goals.

Think big. Start small. Act fast. Entrepreneurs are action oriented and they tend to focus their time and energy on things they can change rather than things they cannot.

Assignment: Reflect on the following questions:

1. What is preventing you from taking the action steps necessary to accomplish your goals?
2. Are the barriers external, such as lack of knowledge and resources, time and money? Or are they internal barriers such as complacency, fear or a lack of confidence?
3. What stands out to you, feels new to you, excites you, or challenges you from this lesson?

Your reflection should demonstrate evidence of in-depth reflective thinking. Your viewpoints and interpretations should be insightful and supported by clear examples.

_____
_____
_____
_____
_____
_____
_____
_____
_____
_____
_____
_____
_____
_____
_____
_____
_____
_____

LESSON 4: PURSUIT OF KNOWLEDGE

Uncle Cleve's Message

Although Uncle Cleve had little formal education, he was a wise man who understood the value of knowledge and was not afraid to learn. He was a curious man and he understood the power of knowledge and the clear connection between knowledge, effort and reward. He developed an insatiable curiosity about the world around him, and for Uncle Cleve, learning became a self-directed, lifelong pursuit. Rather than accepting his lack of formal education as a limitation, he sought knowledge wherever he could find it. Rather than spend his idle time carelessly, he constantly searched for answers, his mind perpetually engaged. An avid reader, he sought knowledge and insight from others. He was an observant man who became a lifelong student, as well as a teacher. He was also open-minded, willing to challenge his own assumptions, as well as the commonly held beliefs of those around him.

Overview

Our effort can only take us as far as our understanding. Entrepreneurs are self-directed, life-long learners who understand the power of knowledge combined with effort. Participants learn how entrepreneurs find the knowledge they need, combining traditional classroom learning with real-world interaction and observation, experimentation and adaptation.

1. The Power of Knowledge
In chapter one, we will explore the power of knowledge combined with effort.

2. Learning Defined
In chapter two, we'll define formal learning and examine its relevance to an entrepreneur.

3. The "aha" Moment
In chapter three, we'll describe the "aha" moment that awakens our curiosity and ignites an innate desire to learn.

4. Planning for Success
In chapter four, we'll discuss the importance of planning. We'll see how entrepreneurs learn by doing, often taking a ready-fire-aim approach.

5. A Word of Caution

In chapter five, we'll discuss the importance of approaching our ideas as unproven assumptions rather than established facts.

6. Knowledge as a Barrier

In chapter six, we'll look at the learning curve and discuss knowledge as a barrier that stops many in their tracks.

7. Learning Redefined

In chapter seven, we'll describe the process of informal learning. We'll see how entrepreneurs learn to find the knowledge they need to get where they want to go.

Lesson Objectives

Our effort can only take us as far as our understanding. Entrepreneurs are self-directed, life-long learners who understand the power of knowledge combined with effort.

After completing Lesson 4, participants will be able to:

- Describe the relationship between knowledge and effort in advancing one's goals.
- Distinguish between formal and informal learning opportunities, and give examples of entrepreneurs making choices to incorporate both.
- Illustrate the "aha" moment concept by describing an external experience that ignited an internal desire to learn.
- Describe a planning vs. a "ready, aim, fire" approach. Evaluate the potential outcomes of each for entrepreneurial success.
- Explain the importance of experimentation and maintaining an open mind in making distinctions between beliefs, assumptions, and facts.
- Develop a self-created curriculum of formal and informal learning opportunities.
- Understand how concepts from this lesson can support college success.

Chalkboard Notes, Part 1

Student-Generated Discussion, Part 1

Once you have viewed this part of the Chalkboard Lesson, think about the core concepts contained in each lesson and create 1 or 2 questions or topics that you would like to discuss in class. Also, write a brief response to one of the following four prompts prior to the next in-class session.

1. Which concept from this Chalkboard Lesson was most intriguing to you? Why?
2. Which entrepreneur's comments most sparked your interest in this lesson? Why?
3. How do the concepts in this lesson apply to an entrepreneurial mindset?
4. How does this portion of Uncle Cleve's story resonate with your own life?

Submit your discussion questions and responses to your facilitator prior to the corresponding in-class session.

In-Class Discussion Notes, Part 1

Chalkboard Notes, Part 2

Student-Generated Discussion, Part 2

Once you have viewed this part of the Chalkboard Lesson, think about the core concepts contained in each lesson and create 1 or 2 questions or topics that you would like to discuss in class. Also, write a brief response to one of the following four prompts prior to the next in-class session.

1. Which concept from this Chalkboard Lesson was most intriguing to you? Why?
2. Which entrepreneur's comments most sparked your interest in this lesson? Why?
3. How do the concepts in this lesson apply to an entrepreneurial mindset?
4. How does this portion of Uncle Cleve's story resonate with your own life?

Submit your discussion questions and responses to your facilitator prior to the corresponding in-class session.

In-Class Discussion Notes, Part 2

103

Application Assignment

Reflecting on your first out-of-the-building assignment, how has the knowledge that you have acquired changed your original assumptions about the problem you intend to solve? What adjustments need to be made? What additional knowledge is required?

In this assignment, you will continue to search for a problem-solution fit. However, you will now look beyond potential customers and search for additional information from other sources of knowledge.

Group Assignment: Identify additional sources of knowledge in your general area of interest (besides potential customers) that will help you better understand the problem you are trying to solve, as well as what solutions, if any, currently exist. Each group member must utilize at least one out-of-the-building source and one Academic Knowledge Source to acquire new knowledge about your idea.

Out-of-the-Building Knowledge Sources (Choose 1)

1. Experienced entrepreneurs.
2. Small business owners.
3. Industry experts.

Academic Knowledge Sources (Choose 1)

1. Online resources (accredited informational websites, online academic journals, newspaper articles, reputable blogs).
2. Print resources (books, encyclopedias, manuals).
3. Academic advisers.

Engage with your Knowledge Source:

- Evaluate what specific information you can acquire from each source.
- Is this source reputable? Why or Why not?
- What solutions, if any, currently exist? Are the existing solutions adequate?
- How might you offer a better solution?

Group Directive: As a group, take notes and document your results in a new version of your revised Opportunity Discovery Canvas. Revise and complete boxes 1 through 3 of the Opportunity Discovery Canvas.

Note: Those who already have a potential solution may complete additional boxes within the opportunity discovery canvas.

Back of the Canvas Analysis: Complete the Notes section on the backside of the Canvas worksheet (approximately 100-150 words). In the "Additional Analysis" section of your notes, consider the following questions:

- What are the greatest obstacles that you must overcome to solve this problem?
- Are you confident that this is a problem worth solving? Why?
- What, if anything, surprised you the most from this experience?

Ice House Opportunity Discovery Canvas

1. Describe the problem you want to solve.	2. Describe the type of people who have this problem.	3. How are they currently solving the problem?

PROBLEM

4. Describe your proposed solution.	5. How will your solution be different?	6. Will people pay for your solution?

SOLUTION

7. How will potential customers know about your solution?	8. How will potential customers purchase your solution?	9. Why will potential customers purchase your solution?

CONNECTION

NOTES

1. What have you learned and how has your idea changed in the most recent version of your canvas? Which of your assumptions were accurate and which of them have changed?

    _____
    _____
    _____
    _____
    _____
    _____
    _____

2. What are your next action steps? Who do you still need to talk to and what knowledge gaps still need to be filled? How can you test your assumptions in the real world with limited time, money, and resources?

    _____
    _____
    _____
    _____
    _____
    _____
    _____

3. Additional Analysis

    _____
    _____
    _____
    _____
    _____
    _____
    _____
    _____
    _____
    _____
    _____

Application Assignment Rubric

Criteria	3	2	1	0
QUANTITY & ACCOUNTABILITY Central questions and directives in the assignment are addressed	☐ Each team member utilizes more than one "Out of the Building" and one "Academic" knowledge source (INDIVIDUAL) ☐ Boxes 1 – 3 of the Opportunity Discovery Canvas are revised based on insights from the knowledge sources ☐ Notes section on the back side of the canvas worksheet and Additional Analysis is completed (approximately 100-150 words) ☐ Assignment is submitted on time	☐ Each team member utilizes at least one "Out of the Building" and one "Academic" knowledge source (INDIVIDUAL) ☐ Boxes 1 – 3 of the Opportunity Discovery canvas are revised based on insights from the knowledge sources ☐ Notes section on the back side of the canvas worksheet is completed (approximately 100-150 words) ☐ Assignment is submitted on time	☐ Each team member utilizes at least one "Out of the Building" and one "Academic" knowledge source (INDIVIDUAL) ☐ Boxes 1 – 3 of the Opportunity Discovery Canvas are revised based on insights from the interviews ☐ Notes section on the back side of the canvas worksheet is completed	☐ Individuals do not utilize knowledge sources ☐ Canvas is not revised
QUALITY & CONNECTION Information sources are relevant, and assignment demonstrates critical thinking skills	☐ Additional knowledge sources help with understanding the problem-solution fit. ☐ Additional knowledge sources are reputable ☐ Team has selected from a diversity of knowledge sources ☐ Team members take and share notes based on assignment questions to engage knowledge sources (INDIVIDUAL) ☐ Canvas revisions are justified and explained by evidence from knowledge sources ☐ Potential solution created and canvas boxes 4 - 6 are also filled in (Optional). ☐ Notes section address changes in the most recent canvas iteration and adjustments to previous assumptions ☐ Next action steps make sense to fill gaps in knowledge. ☐ Additional Analysis in Notes addresses assignment questions	☐ Additional knowledge sources help with understanding the problem-solution fit. ☐ Additional knowledge sources are reputable ☐ Team members take notes gleaned from knowledge sources (INDIVIDUAL) ☐ Canvas revisions are supported by evidence from knowledge sources ☐ Notes section directly address changes in the most recent canvas iteration. ☐ Next action steps are concrete and timely.	☐ The majority of potential customers interviewed have a stake in the canvas problem or solution posed (INDIVIDUAL) ☐ Interview questions are drawn from suggested question set (INDIVIDUAL) ☐ Canvas revisions are made, but evidence to support revisions may be limited, or not convincingly applied ☐ New and/or old ideas may be written in Notes, but are not directly compared ☐ Next action steps are minimal or not well thought through	☐ Individuals do not utilize knowledge sources ☐ Canvas is not revised

Peer Workshop Notes

Reflection Assignment

Reflection Assignments are designed to encourage you to write reflectively about what you are learning and to explore ideas more deeply. These assignments also provide an opportunity to think about the future you want to create for yourself and how best to apply the knowledge you have gained in a way that will enable you to accomplish your goals.

Our effort can only take us as far as our understanding. Entrepreneurs are self-directed, life-long learners who understand the power of knowledge combined with effort.

Assignment: Reflect on the following questions:

1. What subjects, topics or issues interest you most?
2. What is the most effective way for you to learn?
3. If the lack of knowledge is a barrier to you, how can you acquire the knowledge you need to be successful in school and in life?
4. What stands out to you, feels new to you, excites you, or challenges you from this lesson?

Your reflection should demonstrate evidence of in-depth reflective thinking. Your viewpoints and interpretations should be insightful and supported by clear examples.

_____
_____
_____
_____
_____
_____
_____
_____
_____
_____
_____
_____
_____
_____
_____
_____

113

LESSON 5: CREATING WEALTH

Uncle Cleve's Message

Uncle Cleve was internally driven and he understood that his choices and actions rather than his circumstances would ultimately determine the outcome of his life. It was this fundamental shift in his perspective that separated him from others. It was a subtle, yet profound transformation that empowered him to succeed. He spent his time and energy only on things that would improve his life in the long term and lead him toward his goal. His approach to money was no different. Rather than spending his money to buy unnecessary things or to impress others, Uncle Cleve saw money as a tool to invest in his future, a tool that would enable him to create wealth. He was future-focused and willing to make sacrifices to get where he wanted to go. He was willing to live beneath his means because he valued financial freedom (his goal) more than he valued the opinions of others.

Temptations surrounded him just as they did others, yet he developed the ability to subordinate an impulse to a higher value—to his goals, his hopes, and his dreams. He did not drive expensive cars nor eat in fancy restaurants. He avoided the credit trap that so many others fell into. His shoes were old and his clothes were worn yet he took money to the bank and his deposits always exceeded his expenses. And while his money accumulated in the bank, his mind was focused on his next opportunity. Rather than being paid by the hour in a job where someone else controlled his future, Uncle Cleve was focused on solving problems and creating value for others and he understood that he could do that by focusing on saving his income. That way, when an opportunity presented itself, he had the resources to take action.

Overview

Spending or investing? For most, it's not the lack of money that prevents us from prospering. Participants learn fundamental concepts of financial literacy from an entrepreneurial perspective. Learn how entrepreneurs manage their expenses, handle credit and leverage their abilities to create sustainable wealth.

1. Wealth Perceived
In chapter one, we'll examine some of the common misconceptions about wealth, as well as the underlying beliefs and assumptions that so often lead us astray.

2. Wealth Defined
In chapter two, we'll define the four basic concepts that become the foundation for creating wealth.

3. Spending vs. Investing

In chapter three, we'll explore the fundamental difference between spending and investing when it comes to creating wealth.

4. The Credit Trap

In chapter four, we'll learn how to use credit as a lever to advance our goals rather than a burden that keeps us stuck.

5. An Entrepreneur's Approach

In chapter five, we'll see how entrepreneurs like Uncle Cleve create sustainable wealth regardless of the circumstances from which they begin.

Lesson Objectives

Spending or investing? For most, it's not the lack of money that prevents us from prospering.

After completing Lesson 5, participants will be able to:

- ■ Describe the different mindsets that support the appearance of wealth vs. the actual creation of wealth.
- ■ Define and give examples of income, expense, asset, liability, and equity.
- ■ Analyze a simple balance sheet and identify the owner's equity.
- ■ Describe the difference between spending and investing.
- ■ Evaluate a credit decision for its ability to either leverage and advance goals or create a financial burden.
- ■ Describe an entrepreneur's approach to creating wealth and cite real-world examples.
- ■ Understand how concepts from this lesson can support college success

Chalkboard Notes, Part 1

Student-Generated Discussion, Part 1

Once you have viewed this part of the Chalkboard Lesson, think about the core concepts contained in each lesson and create 1 or 2 questions or topics that you would like to discuss in class. Also, write a brief response to one of the following four prompts prior to the next in-class session.

1. Which concept from this Chalkboard Lesson was most intriguing to you? Why?
2. Which entrepreneur's comments most sparked your interest in this lesson? Why?
3. How do the concepts in this lesson apply to an entrepreneurial mindset?
4. How does this portion of Uncle Cleve's story resonate with your own life?

Submit your discussion questions and responses to your facilitator prior to the corresponding in-class session.

_____
_____
_____
_____
_____
_____
_____
_____
_____
_____
_____
_____
_____
_____
_____
_____
_____
_____
_____
_____
_____
_____
_____
_____
_____

In-Class Discussion Notes, Part 1

Chalkboard Notes, Part 2

Student-Generated Discussion, Part 2

Once you have viewed this part of the Chalkboard Lesson, think about the core concepts contained in each lesson and create 1 or 2 questions or topics that you would like to discuss in class. Also, write a brief response to one of the following four prompts prior to the next in-class session.

1. Which concept from this Chalkboard Lesson was most intriguing to you? Why?
2. Which entrepreneur's comments most sparked your interest in this lesson? Why?
3. How do the concepts in this lesson apply to an entrepreneurial mindset?
4. How does this portion of Uncle Cleve's story resonate with your own life?

Submit your discussion questions and responses to your facilitator prior to the corresponding in-class session.

In-Class Discussion Notes, Part 2

Application Assignment

Now that you have taken the time to better understand the problem, it's time to shift your focus towards a solution. In this assignment, you will continue to reinforce the importance of action combined with knowledge as the engine that drives the entrepreneurial process.

Group Assignment: Using what you have learned thus far, document your proposed solution in the latest version of your canvas (boxes 4 through 6).

Now, go back out of the building. Identify and interview your potential customers and other stakeholders who may benefit from your proposed solution. This may include people you have already talked to about your idea, as well as additional new customers and stakeholders. Each group member must interview a minimum of 10 potential customers or stakeholders.

Engage the potential customer or stakeholder:

- Communicate your proposed solution and listen to their feedback.
- Ask specific questions drawn from boxes 4 through 6, using the canvas as a guide.
- If necessary, revisit questions you asked in previous assignments.
- Ask if they know of an additional person or knowledge resource that might help you with your idea.

Group Directive: As a group, take notes and document your results in a new version of your revised Opportunity Discovery Canvas. Revise and complete boxes 1 through 6 of the Opportunity Discovery Canvas.

Back of the Canvas Analysis: Complete the Notes section on the back side of the canvas worksheet (approximately 100-150 words). In the "Additional Analysis" section of your Notes, consider the following questions:

- How would you rate your customers' level of interest in your solution? (Strongly interested, somewhat interested, not interested, unclear?)
- Are you confident in your proposed solution or do adjustments need to be made?

Note: Your group should also begin to prepare for the midterm canvas presentations.

Ice House Opportunity Discovery Canvas

1. Describe the problem you want to solve.	2. Describe the type of people who have this problem.	3. How are they currently solving the problem?

PROBLEM

4. Describe your proposed solution.	5. How will your solution be different?	6. Will people pay for your solution?

SOLUTION

7. How will potential customers know about your solution?	8. How will potential customers purchase your solution?	9. Why will potential customers purchase your solution?

CONNECTION

NOTES

1. What have you learned and how has your idea changed in the most recent version of your canvas? Which of your assumptions were accurate and which of them have changed?

     _____

     _____

     _____

     _____

     _____

     _____

     _____

2. What are your next action steps? Who do you still need to talk to and what knowledge gaps still need to be filled? How can you test your assumptions in the real world with limited time, money, and resources?

     _____

     _____

     _____

     _____

     _____

     _____

     _____

3. Additional Analysis

     _____

     _____

     _____

     _____

     _____

     _____

     _____

     _____

     _____

     _____

     _____

Application Assignment Rubric

Score / Criteria	3	2	1	0
QUANTITY & ACCOUNTABILITY Central questions and directives in the assignment are addressed	☐ Boxes 4 – 6 of the Opportunity Discovery Canvas are documented with a proposed solution ☐ Each team member conducts face-to-face interviews with at least 10 potential customers (INDIVIDUAL) ☐ Boxes 1 – 6 of the Canvas are revised based on insights from the interviews ☐ Notes section on the back side of the Canvas worksheet is completed (approximately 100-150 words) ☐ Additional Analysis section of Notes is completed ☐ Assignment is submitted on time	☐ Boxes 4 – 6 of the Opportunity Discovery Canvas are documented with a proposed solution ☐ Each team member conducts face-to-face interviews with at least 10 potential customers (INDIVIDUAL) ☐ Boxes 1 – 6 of the canvas are revised based on insights from the interviews ☐ Notes section on the back side of the canvas worksheet is completed (approximately 100-150 words) ☐ Assignment is submitted on time	☐ Boxes 4 – 6 of the Opportunity Discovery Canvas are documented with a proposed solution ☐ Some team members do not conduct at least 10 interviews (INDIVIDUAL) ☐ Boxes 1 – 6 of the Opportunity Discovery Canvas are revised based on insights from the interviews ☐ Notes section on the back side of the canvas worksheet is completed	☐ Individuals do not conduct interviews ☐ Canvas is not revised
QUALITY & CONNECTION Information sources are relevant, and assignment demonstrates critical thinking skills	☐ Proposed solution documented in boxes 4 – 6 of canvas describes an actionable fit with problems outlined in boxes 1 - 3 ☐ Potential customers interviewed clearly have a stake in the canvas solution posed (INDIVIDUAL) ☐ Complete question set is addressed during interviews (INDIVIDUAL) ☐ Canvas revisions are justified and explained with supporting details, examples, and evidence from interviews ☐ Notes section address changes in the most recent canvas iteration and adjustments to previous assumptions ☐ Next action steps make sense to fill gaps in knowledge and continue discovery process ☐ Additional Analysis is justified with interview evidence	☐ Proposed solution documented in boxes 4 – 6 of canvas describes a fit with problems outlined in boxes 1 - 3 ☐ Potential customers interviewed clearly have a stake in the canvas solution posed (INDIVIDUAL) ☐ Interview questions are drawn from suggested question set (INDIVIDUAL) ☐ Canvas revisions are justified with supporting evidence from interviews ☐ Notes section addresses basic changes in the most recent canvas iteration. ☐ Next action steps are concrete and logical.	☐ Proposed solution documented in boxes 4 – 6 of canvas references problems outlined in boxes 1 - 3 ☐ The majority of potential customers interviewed have a stake in the canvas solution posed (INDIVIDUAL) ☐ Interview questions are drawn from suggested question set (INDIVIDUAL) ☐ Canvas revisions are made, but evidence to support revisions may be limited, or not convincingly applied ☐ New and/or old ideas may be written in Notes, but are not directly compared ☐ Next action steps are minimal or not well thought through	☐ Individuals do not conduct interviews ☐ Canvas is not revised

Peer Workshop Notes

Reflection Assignment

Reflection assignments are designed to encourage you to write reflectively about what you are learning and to explore ideas more deeply. These assignments also provide an opportunity to think about the future you want to create for yourself and how best to apply the knowledge you have gained in a way that will enable you to accomplish your goals.

Spending or investing? For most, it's not the lack of money that prevents us from prospering. Entrepreneurs learn to manage their expenses, handle credit and leverage their abilities to create sustainable wealth, regardless of where they start.

Assignment: Reflect on the following questions:

1. Is the ability to create wealth important to you? Why or why not?
2. How do your beliefs affect your ability create wealth?
3. What is the greatest barrier to creating wealth that stands in your way?
4. What stands out to you, feels new to you, excites you, or challenges you from this lesson?

Your reflection should demonstrate evidence of in-depth reflective thinking. Your viewpoints and interpretations should be insightful and supported by clear examples.

_____

_____

_____

_____

_____

_____

_____

_____

_____

_____

_____

_____

_____

_____

_____

_____

_____

_____

135

Midterm Presentation

Assignment: Thus far, you have been out of the building testing your ideas with potential customers and finding knowledge through a variety of resources. Now your group will have the opportunity to communicate your ideas in a formal presentation. This will enable you to demonstrate the evolution of your ideas, answer any questions and receive feedback from your peers.

Guidelines: Your presentation should be no more than 3-5 minutes long, so be sure to communicate your ideas clearly and concisely. You may use a PowerPoint presentation, various drafts of the Opportunity Discovery Canvas or other visual aids in your presentation. However, it is important to remember that visual aids should complement, rather than replace, face-to-face communication.

Once your presentation is complete, an additional 3-5 minutes should be set aside for peers' questions and feedback. We strongly suggest that all members of the group participate in the presentation. For more details on grading criteria for these presentations, consult the presentation rubric.

Group Directive: Using canvas boxes 1 through 6 as a guide, clearly and concisely address the following questions in your group presentation. Provide specific examples from your Opportunity Discovery Process thus far:

1. What was your original idea?
2. How has your idea changed throughout customer interviews from your out-of-the-building experience?
3. Who did you interview and how did you find them? Why did you identify them as potential customers?
4. What else did you learn from academic and other out-of-the-building knowledge sources?
5. What are the most important action steps that will move you closer to a finding a problem-solution fit?

When your presentation is over, listen attentively to the other presentations and provide constructive feedback to your peers. After all, collaboration is key to developing new ideas and improving your problem-solution fit.

Midterm Presentation Rubric

Score / Criteria	3	2	1	0
QUANTITY & ACCOUNTABILITY Central questions and directives in the assignment are addressed	☐ Presentation is 3 – 5 minutes long ☐ Facilitated question and answer follow up is 3 – 5 minutes long ☐ All members of the team participate in the presentation and demonstrate shared understand of the group's canvas Process ☐ Content for pitch is drawn from canvas boxes 1 - 6	☐ Presentation is 3 – 5 minutes long ☐ Facilitated question and answer follow up is 3 – 5 minutes long ☐ All members of the team participate in the presentation and demonstrate shared understanding of the group's canvas Process ☐ Content for pitch is drawn from canvas boxes 1 - 6	☐ Presentation is 3 – 5 minutes long ☐ Question and answer follow up takes place ☐ Most members of the team participate in the presentation. Individual participation of all team members is uneven ☐ Content for pitch is drawn from canvas boxes 1 - 6	☐ Does not present
QUALITY & CONNECTION Content is derived from canvas search process, and assignment demonstrates critical thinking and presentation skills	☐ Presentation demonstrates professionalism through evidence of design, logical flow, preparation and practice ☐ PowerPoints or other visual graphic aids enhance the speakers' message ☐ Ideas are communicated clearly and concisely ☐ Original canvas idea and subsequent evolution of idea is explained ☐ Who was interviewed and why is explained ☐ Specific examples from the Opportunity Discovery Process support all aspects of the presentation, with relevant details from interviews with potential customers or other knowledge sources to justify changes in idea ☐ Next action steps in seeking a problem-solution fit are outlined ☐ Questions and feedback from peers are respectfully received and competently answered	☐ Presentation demonstrates professionalism through evidence of design, preparation and practice ☐ Team's enthusiasm engages audience ☐ Visual graphic aids enhance the speakers' message, rather than distracting from it ☐ Presentation expands upon the ideas and observations shared at the midterm ☐ Changes in the idea are reported, and follow directly from knowledge gained through Opportunity Discovery Process (customer interviews and other knowledge sources) ☐ Next action steps beyond course are outlined ☐ Questions and feedback are respectfully received and competently answered	☐ Presentation delivery is informal and lacks logical organization ☐ Individual participation of all team members is uneven ☐ Ideas may ramble or be underdeveloped ☐ Original idea is present ☐ Changes in idea are reported, but cause and effect links to knowledge gained from Opportunity Discovery Process may be unclear ☐ Specific examples from Opportunity Discovery Process are shared, but may not convincingly support canvas evolution ☐ Next action steps may or may not be outlined ☐ Questions and feedback from peers are respectfully received and answered	☐ Does not present

LESSON 6: BUILDING YOUR BRAND

Uncle Cleve's Message

Uncle Cleve understood that problems were opportunities. He knew that if he could solve problems for other people, he could also empower himself. He also understood the power of being reliable and that his reputation was an essential aspect of his ability to succeed. He also comprehended that it was an aspect of his life that he could control. Central to Uncle Cleve's success as an entrepreneur was the simple fact that he was reliable. The people in Glen Allan, Mississippi knew they could count on him. They trusted him to solve their problems. They knew his word was his bond. They knew he neither gave nor accepted excuses. They knew they could set their clocks to Uncle Cleve. Uncle Cleve had no patents to protect his ideas. His word was his "intellectual property." Reliability was his brand. It was the promise he made to his customers.

The more people who knew that they could count on Cleve, the more opportunities he found. They not only trusted him to deliver ice, they also bought wood and coal from him in the winter and they allowed him to repair their high-dollar cars. It was his commitment to his word that gave him confidence. It put the lift in his stride and the twinkle in his eye. Uncle Cleve was intrinsically motivated, and his reputation was something he could control. Although it would have been easy for him to do otherwise, Uncle Cleve did not discriminate. He treated everyone fairly. Even when he faced a situation where humiliation seemed the only outcome, Uncle Cleve managed to maintain his dignity. He refused, taking the high road and refusing to lower himself to someone else's dismal standards. By doing what he said he would do, rain or shine, he watched his business grow.

Overview

Actions speak louder than words. Entrepreneurs are problem solvers and reliability is the key to their success. Using case studies and modern-day examples, participants learn how entrepreneurs transform simple solutions into big opportunities by building a reputation for reliability.

1. Brand Defined
In chapter one, we'll define the term brand in a way that is relevant and actionable to an aspiring entrepreneur.

2. Defining your Brand
In chapter two, we'll discuss the importance of understanding your customers as the key to defining your brand.

3. Communicating your Brand

In chapter three, we'll learn how entrepreneurs communicate their brand through their words, as well as their actions. We'll also see how they leverage their brand to overcome inertia and communicate value to potential customers.

4. Building your Brand

In chapter four, we'll learn how entrepreneurs build their brand. You'll learn firsthand how they transform simple solutions into sustainable successes by being consistent and reliable.

5. Confidence

In chapter five, we'll examine the role of confidence, where it comes from and why it is important.

Lesson Objectives

Actions speak louder than words. Entrepreneurs are problem solvers and reliability is the key to their success.

After completing Lesson 6, participants will be able to:

- Define brand using the concepts of reputation, reliability, actions and words.
- Describe how a focus on solving problems creates a brand identity.
- Describe the importance of seeking to understand before being understood.
- Give examples of explicit and implicit messages.
- List characteristics of a customer experience that can build a valued brand.
- Understand how concepts from this lesson can support college success.

Chalkboard Notes, Part 1

Student-Generated Discussion, Part 1

Once you have viewed this part of the Chalkboard Lesson, think about the core concepts contained in each lesson and create 1 or 2 questions or topics that you would like to discuss in class. Also, write a brief response to one of the following four prompts prior to the next in-class session.

1. Which concept from this Chalkboard Lesson was most intriguing to you? Why?
2. Which entrepreneur's comments most sparked your interest in this lesson? Why?
3. How do the concepts in this lesson apply to an entrepreneurial mindset?
4. How does this portion of Uncle Cleve's story resonate with your own life?

Submit your discussion questions and responses to your facilitator prior to the corresponding in-class session.

_____

_____

_____

_____

_____

_____

_____

_____

_____

_____

_____

_____

_____

_____

_____

_____

_____

_____

_____

_____

_____

_____

_____

_____

In-Class Discussion Notes, Part 1

Chalkboard Notes, Part 2

Student-Generated Discussion, Part 2

Once you have viewed this part of the Chalkboard Lesson, think about the core concepts contained in each lesson and create 1 or 2 questions or topics that you would like to discuss in class. Also, write a brief response to one of the following four prompts prior to the next in-class session.

1. Which concept from this Chalkboard Lesson was most intriguing to you? Why?
2. Which entrepreneur's comments most sparked your interest in this lesson? Why?
3. How do the concepts in this lesson apply to an entrepreneurial mindset?
4. How does this portion of Uncle Cleve's story resonate with your own life?

Submit your discussion questions and responses to your facilitator prior to the corresponding in-class session.

_____

_____

_____

_____

_____

_____

_____

_____

_____

_____

_____

_____

_____

_____

_____

_____

_____

_____

_____

_____

_____

In-Class Discussion Notes, Part 2

149

Application Assignment

Now that you are familiar with the Opportunity Discovery Process, it's time to accelerate the learning process. In previous assignments you have used canvas boxes 1 through 6 to help guide your search for confirmation of a problem-solution fit. Once you are confident that people will pay for your product or service, it's time to focus on canvas boxes 7 through 9. Here, you will begin to think about how you can connect with a broader audience of potential customers and stakeholders.

Group Assignment: This assignment consists of two objectives. Each individual group member can choose to complete Objective 1 or Objective 2. At least one group member must complete Objective 1 and at least one group member must complete Objective 2.

Objective 1
Identify and interview 10 more of your potential customers and other stakeholders.

Engage the potential customer or stakeholder:

- Communicate your proposed solution and listen to their feedback.
- Using the canvas as a guide, ask specific questions drawn from boxes 7 through 9.
- If necessary, revisit questions you asked in previous assignments.
- Ask if they know of an additional person or knowledge resource that might help you with your idea.

Objective 2
Identify additional sources of knowledge in your general area of interest (besides potential customers) that will help you solve the unanswered questions outlined in boxes 7 through 9 of your Opportunity Discovery Canvas.

Evaluate what specific information you can acquire from each source of knowledge. Each group member must utilize at least one out-of-the-building knowledge source, as well as one academic knowledge source to gather new knowledge about your idea.

Out of the Building Knowledge Sources (Choose 1)

1. Experienced entrepreneurs.
2. Small business owners.
3. Industry experts.

Academic Knowledge Sources (Choose 1)

1. Online resources (accredited informational websites, online academic journals, newspaper articles, reputable blogs).
2. Print resources (books, encyclopedias, manuals).
3. Academic advisers.

Engage with your Knowledge Source:

- Evaluate what specific information you can acquire from each source.
- How do similar businesses communicate with their customers and deliver their solution?
- How is your idea unique from the products or services of existing businesses?
- Identify additional knowledge sources (people or other resources) you know of that might be able to help you accomplish your goals.

Group Directive: As a group, take notes and document your results in a new version of your revised Opportunity Discovery Canvas. Revise and complete boxes 1 through 9 of the Opportunity Discovery Canvas.

Back of the Canvas Analysis: Complete the "Notes" section on the backside of the canvas worksheet (approximately 100-150 words). In the "Additional Analysis" section of your Notes, consider the following questions:

- How would you rate your customers' level of interest in your revised solution? (Strongly interested, somewhat interested, not interested, unclear, etc.)
- Are you confident in your proposed solution or do adjustments need to be made?
- Are there enough customers to make your efforts worthwhile?
- Do you need to revise the way you communicate your message based on customer feedback?

 Ice House Opportunity Discovery Canvas

1. Describe the problem you want to solve.

2. Describe the type of people who have this problem.

3. How are they currently solving the problem?

PROBLEM

4. Describe your proposed solution.

5. How will your solution be different?

6. Will people pay for your solution?

SOLUTION

7. How will potential customers know about your solution?

8. How will potential customers purchase your solution?

9. Why will potential customers purchase your solution?

CONNECTION

NOTES

1. What have you learned and how has your idea changed in the most recent version of your canvas? Which of your assumptions were accurate and which of them have changed?

_____
_____
_____
_____
_____
_____
_____

2. What are your next action steps? Who do you still need to talk to and what knowledge gaps still need to be filled? How can you test your assumptions in the real world with limited time, money, and resources?

_____
_____
_____
_____
_____
_____
_____

3. Additional Analysis

_____
_____
_____
_____
_____
_____
_____
_____
_____
_____
_____
_____

Application Assignment Rubric

Score / Criteria	3	2	1	0
QUANTITY & ACCOUNTABILITY Central questions and directives in the assignment are addressed	☐ Each team member conducts face-to-face interviews with at least 10 potential customers (INDIVIDUAL) **OR** Each team member utilizes more than one "Out of the Building" and one "Academic" knowledge source (INDIVIDUAL) ☐ Boxes 1 – 9 of the Opportunity Discovery Canvas are revised based on interviews and other knowledge sources ☐ Notes section on the back side of the canvas worksheet is completed (approximately 100-150 words) ☐ Assignment is submitted on time	☐ Each team member conducts face-to-face interviews with at least 10 potential customers (INDIVIDUAL) **OR** Each team member utilizes at least one "Out of the Building" and one "Academic" knowledge source (INDIVIDUAL) ☐ Boxes 1 – 9 of the Opportunity Discovery Canvas are revised based on interviews and other knowledge sources ☐ Notes section on the back side of the canvas worksheet is completed (approximately 100-150 words) ☐ Assignment is submitted on time	☐ Some team members do not conduct at least 10 interviews OR utilize at least two knowledge sources (one "Out of the Building" and one "Academic") (INDIVIDUAL) ☐ Boxes 1 – 9 of the Opportunity Discovery Canvas are revised based on the interviews ☐ Notes section on the back side of the canvas worksheet is completed	☐ Individuals do not conduct interviews or utilize knowledge sources ☐ Canvas is not revised
QUALITY & CONNECTION Information sources are relevant, and assignment demonstrates critical thinking skills	☐ Documentation in boxes 7 - 9 of canvas outlines actionable connection to broad scope of customers ☐ A broader audience of potential customers are interviewed (INDIVIDUAL) ☐ Knowledge sources are chosen to gain broader context and comparative models for your idea (INDIVIDUAL) ☐ Canvas revisions for boxes 1 – 9 are justified and explained by supporting details, examples, and evidence from interviews and knowledge sources ☐ Notes section address changes in the most recent canvas iteration and adjustments to previous assumptions ☐ Next action steps fill gaps in knowledge and continue discovery process ☐ Additional Analysis is justified with interview evidence	☐ Proposed solution documented in boxes 4 – 6 of canvas describes a fit with problems outlined in boxes 1 – 3 ☐ Potential customers interviewed clearly have a stake in the canvas solution posed (INDIVIDUAL) ☐ Interview questions are drawn from suggested question set (INDIVIDUAL) ☐ Canvas revisions are justified and explained with supporting evidence from interviews ☐ Notes section addresses basic changes in the most recent canvas iteration. ☐ Next action steps are concrete and logical.	☐ Documentation is expanded to include canvas boxes 7 - 9 ☐ The majority of potential customers interviewed and knowledge sources utilized go beyond previous sources to make broader connections (INDIVIDUAL) ☐ Canvas revisions are made, but evidence to support revisions may be limited, or not convincingly applied ☐ New and/or old ideas may be written in Notes, but are not directly compared ☐ Next action steps are minimal or not well thought through	☐ Individuals do not conduct interviews or utilize knowledge sources ☐ Canvas is not revised

Peer Workshop Notes

Reflection Assignment

Reflection assignments are designed to encourage you to write reflectively about what you are learning and to explore ideas more deeply. These assignments also provide an opportunity to think about the future you want to create for yourself and how best to apply the knowledge you have gained in a way that will enable you to accomplish your goals.

Actions speak louder than words. Entrepreneurs are problem solvers. They learn how to transform simple solutions into big opportunities and reliability is the key.

Assignment: Reflect on the following questions:

1. What does the term "branding" mean to you?
2. How do you want to communicate your personal brand to your peers, academic advisers, mentors and colleagues?
3. How can the concept of branding help you accomplish your personal, academic and professional goals?
4. What stands out to you, feels new to you, excites you, or challenges you from this lesson?

Your reflection should demonstrate evidence of in-depth reflective thinking. Your viewpoints and interpretations should be insightful and supported by clear examples.

159

LESSON 7: CREATING COMMUNITY

Uncle Cleve's Message

Because he was future focused, Uncle Cleve taught himself to stick with others who were the same. He made the choice to create the life he wanted rather than the life everyone around him had accepted. Uncle Cleve chose to focus his time and attention on things he could change, on the aspects of his life over which he had control. He had little time for the juke joints and neighborhood saloons. He did not engage in gossip and small talk. Instead he earned the respect of others and created a community of respect, a network of action-oriented individuals who shared his commitment to success. He earned the respect of others and he paid attention to what other business owners were doing. Uncle Cleve was a student, as well as a teacher. He learned from the success of others and, thankfully, he was willing to pass along what he had learned.

Overview

Entrepreneurs understand the power of positive influence and they learn to surround themselves with others who have been where they intend to go. Participants will learn how to tap into a network of entrepreneurs, mentors and trusted advisors within their own communities.

1. Community Defined
In chapter one, we'll define a community as a success network of others who have been where we want to go.

2. The Value of a Network
In chapter two, we'll discuss the value and the influence that a success network can provide.

3. Who is in our Network?
In chapter three, we'll examine five separate sources of support from those who are on a similar path to successful entrepreneurs who have been where we intend to go.

4. Crossing the Chasm
In chapter four, we'll describe three distinct phases of transformation and the role our success network plays in each.

5. Building a Success Network
And finally, in chapter five, we'll discuss how entrepreneurs create their success networks as well as some of the obstacles that often stand in their way.

Lesson Objectives

Entrepreneurs understand the power of positive influence and they learn to surround themselves with others who have been where they intend to go.

After completing Lesson 7, participants will be able to:

- Describe the role that success networks can play.
- Understand the importance of an intentionally chosen support group.
- Identify and interact with potential mentors and advisors and others who may provide critical guidance and support.
- List and explain the value of the four areas of influence that a network can provide.
- Name the five groups from which success network members can be drawn and describe the type of support each group offers.
- Understand how concepts from this lesson can support college success.

Chalkboard Notes, Part 1

Student-Generated Discussion, Part 1

Once you have viewed this part of the Chalkboard Lesson, think about the core concepts contained in each lesson and create 1 or 2 questions or topics that you would like to discuss in class. Also, write a brief response to one of the following four prompts prior to the next in-class session.

1. Which concept from this Chalkboard Lesson was most intriguing to you? Why?
2. Which entrepreneur's comments most sparked your interest in this lesson? Why?
3. How do the concepts in this lesson apply to an entrepreneurial mindset?
4. How does this portion of Uncle Cleve's story resonate with your own life?

Submit your discussion questions and responses to your facilitator prior to the corresponding in-class session.

In-Class Discussion Notes, Part 1

Chalkboard Notes, Part 2

Student-Generated Discussion, Part 2

Once you have viewed this part of the Chalkboard Lesson, think about the core concepts contained in each lesson and create 1 or 2 questions or topics that you would like to discuss in class. Also, write a brief response to one of the following four prompts prior to the next in-class session.

1. Which concept from this Chalkboard Lesson was most intriguing to you? Why?
2. Which entrepreneur's comments most sparked your interest in this lesson? Why?
3. How do the concepts in this lesson apply to an entrepreneurial mindset?
4. How does this portion of Uncle Cleve's story resonate with your own life?

Submit your discussion questions and responses to your facilitator prior to the corresponding in-class session.

In-Class Discussion Notes, Part 2

171

Application Assignment

In this assignment, we will continue the accelerated Opportunity Discovery Process. In the previous assignment, you focused on connecting with a broader audience of potential customers. Now it's time to take a step back to review your entire canvas and to identify any remaining areas of uncertainty. What additional knowledge is required? Who else can you connect with to provide the knowledge you need?

Group Assignment: Again, this assignment consists of two objectives. Each individual group member can choose to complete Objective 1 or Objective 2. At least one group member must complete Objective 1 and at least one group member must complete Objective 2.

Objective 1
Identify and interview 10 additional potential customers or stakeholders.

Engage the potential customer or stakeholder:

- Communicate your proposed solution and listen to their feedback.
- Using the canvas as a guide, ask specific questions that address any areas of uncertainty with your idea.
- If necessary, revisit questions you asked in previous assignments.

Ask if they can recommend any additional person (potential employees, partners, mentors or professional service-providers) or knowledge resource that might help you with your idea.

Objective 2
Identify additional sources of knowledge (besides potential customers) that will help you solve the most important questions that will confirm a problem-solution fit.

Evaluate what specific information you can acquire from each source of knowledge. Each group member must utilize at least one out-of-the-building knowledge source, as well as one academic knowledge source to acquire new knowledge about your idea.

Out of the Building Knowledge Sources (Choose 1)

1. Experienced entrepreneurs.
2. Small business owners.
3. Industry experts.

Academic Knowledge Sources (Choose 1)

1. Online resources (accredited informational websites, online academic journals, newspaper articles, reputable blogs).
2. Print resources (books, encyclopedias, manuals).
3. Academic advisers.

Engage with your Knowledge Source:

- Evaluate what specific information you can acquire from each source.
- Identify additional knowledge sources (people or other resources) you know of that might be able to help you accomplish your goals.

Group Directive: As a group, take notes and document your results in a new version of your revised Opportunity Discovery Canvas. Revise and complete boxes 1 through 9 of the Opportunity Discovery Canvas.

Back of the Canvas Analysis: Complete the "Notes" section on the backside of the canvas worksheet (approximately 100-150 words). In the "Additional Analysis" section of your Notes, consider the following questions:

- How would you rate your customers' level of interest in your revised solution? (Strongly interested, somewhat interested, not interested, unclear, etc.)
- Are you confident in your proposed solution or do adjustments need to be made?
- Who else should you include in your network? How can these individuals provide new value?

Ice House Opportunity Discovery Canvas

1. Describe the problem you want to solve.	2. Describe the type of people who have this problem.	3. How are they currently solving the problem?

PROBLEM

4. Describe your proposed solution.	5. How will your solution be different?	6. Will people pay for your solution?

SOLUTION

7. How will potential customers know about your solution?	8. How will potential customers purchase your solution?	9. Why will potential customers purchase your solution?

CONNECTION

NOTES

1. What have you learned and how has your idea changed in the most recent version of your canvas? Which of your assumptions were accurate and which of them have changed?

    _____
    _____
    _____
    _____
    _____
    _____
    _____

2. What are your next action steps? Who do you still need to talk to and what knowledge gaps still need to be filled? How can you test your assumptions in the real world with limited time, money, and resources?

    _____
    _____
    _____
    _____
    _____
    _____
    _____

3. Additional Analysis

    _____
    _____
    _____
    _____
    _____
    _____
    _____
    _____
    _____
    _____
    _____

Application Assignment Rubric

Score / Criteria	3	2	1	0
QUANTITY & ACCOUNTABILITY Central questions and directives in the assignment are addressed	☐ Each team member conducts face-to-face interviews with at least 10 potential customers (INDIVIDUAL) **OR** Each team member utilizes more than one "Out of the Building" and one "Academic" knowledge source (INDIVIDUAL) ☐ Boxes 1 – 9 of the Opportunity Discovery Canvas are revised based on interviews and other knowledge sources ☐ Notes section on the back side of the canvas worksheet is completed (approximately 100-150 words) ☐ Assignment is submitted on time	☐ Each team member conducts face-to-face interviews with at least 10 potential customers (INDIVIDUAL) **OR** Each team member utilizes at least one "Out of the Building" and one "Academic" knowledge source (INDIVIDUAL) ☐ Boxes 1 – 9 of the Opportunity Discovery Canvas are revised based on interviews and other knowledge sources ☐ Notes section on the back side of the canvas worksheet is completed (approximately 100-150 words) ☐ Assignment is submitted on time	☐ Some team members do not conduct at least 10 interviews OR utilize at least two knowledge sources (one "Out of the Building" and one "Academic") (INDIVIDUAL) ☐ Boxes 1 – 9 of the Opportunity Discovery Canvas are revised based on the interviews ☐ Notes section on the back side of the canvas worksheet is completed	☐ Individuals do not conduct interviews or utilize knowledge sources ☐ Canvas is not completed
QUALITY & CONNECTION Information sources are relevant, and assignment demonstrates critical thinking skills	☐ Team has developed strategies to respond to remaining areas of uncertainty identified in canvas process ☐ Potential customers interviewed have knowledge about areas of uncertainty (INDIVIDUAL) ☐ Knowledge sources help confirm a problem-solution fit (INDIVIDUAL) ☐ Revisions and completion of canvas boxes 1 – 9 are justified and explained using supporting evidence from interviews and knowledge sources ☐ Notes section directly address changes in the most recent canvas iteration and adjustments to previous assumptions ☐ Next action steps make sense to fill gaps in knowledge and continue discovery process ☐ Additional Analysis is justified with concrete evidence.	☐ Remaining areas of uncertainty are identified in canvas process ☐ Potential customers interviewed have knowledge about areas of uncertainty (INDIVIDUAL) ☐ Knowledge sources address areas of uncertainty (INDIVIDUAL) ☐ Revisions and completion of canvas boxes 1 – 9 are supported by evidence from interviews and knowledge sources ☐ Notes section directly address changes in the most recent canvas iteration. ☐ Next action steps are concrete and timely	☐ Entire canvas has been reviewed with an eye to completion ☐ Many potential customers interviewed and knowledge sources utilized can provide knowledge to complete canvas (INDIVIDUAL) ☐ Revisions and completion of canvas boxes 1 – 9 are made, but evidence to support revisions may be limited, or not convincingly applied ☐ New and/or old ideas may be written in Notes, but are not directly compared ☐ Action steps are minimal or not well thought through ☐ Next action steps are minimal or not well thought through	☐ Individuals do not conduct interviews or utilize knowledge sources ☐ Canvas is not revised

Peer Workshop Notes

Reflection Assignment

Reflection assignments are designed to encourage you to write reflectively about what you are learning and to explore ideas more deeply. These assignments also provide an opportunity to think about the future you want to create for yourself and how best to apply the knowledge you have gained in a way that will enable you to accomplish your goals.

Entrepreneurs understand the power of positive influence and they learn to surround themselves with others who have been where they intend to go.

Assignment: Reflect on the following questions:

1. How do the people around you influence your behavior?
2. Why is it important to develop a success network?
3. Who is currently in your success network? What type of people do you still need to include in your success network?
4. What stands out to you, feels new to you, excites you, or challenges you from this lesson?

Your reflection should demonstrate evidence of in-depth reflective thinking. Your viewpoints and interpretations should be insightful and supported by clear examples.

_____
_____
_____
_____
_____
_____
_____
_____
_____
_____
_____
_____
_____
_____
_____
_____
_____

LESSON 8: THE POWER OF PERSISTENCE

Uncle Cleve's Message

Life was not easy for Uncle Cleve. He worked hard every day. Yet, of all the "secrets" to his success, none is perhaps more powerful than persistence—his refusal to give up. And, like most entrepreneurs, his road to success was not without pitfalls, setbacks, and failures. Yet he knew that he could not fail as long as he refused to quit. While many attribute success to an innate ability, luck, or circumstance, most overlook persistence, a subtle yet powerful mindset that Uncle Cleve surely understood. It is persistence that will enable you to face challenges and overcome obstacles. It is persistence that will empower you to forge ahead in the face of fear and uncertainty and will encourage you to push yourself to find solutions. Like our previous mindset lessons, perseverance is something we can all learn. It does not require specialized knowledge. It does not require a rare ability, an innate talent, or a genius IQ. It does not require access to money, power or privilege. Perseverance and determination are traits we are all capable of. And, more often than not, perseverance is the key to creating success.

Overview

Entrepreneurship is not "get rich quick" and expecting it to be easy is a mistake. The "secret" behind every entrepreneur's success is hard work, perseverance and determination. Participants learn from experience the importance of persistence and the role it plays in every entrepreneur's success story.

    1. Dawn Halfaker - "Focus on what you have"

    2. Brian Scudamore - "Slow and steady wins the race"

    3. Ted and Sirena Moore - "Are you willing to go the distance?"

    4. Rodney Walker - "Imagine something greater"

    5. Jason Campbell - "Adversity as an advantage"

    6. Palwasha Siddiqi - "Nothing in life is easy"

    7. Ryan Blair - "A poor kid with poor beliefs"

    8. David Petite - "Create your own reality"

Lesson Objectives

Entrepreneurship is not about how to "get rich quick" and expecting it to be easy is a mistake. The so-called secret behind every entrepreneur's success is hard work, perseverance, and determination.

After completing Lesson 8, participants will be able to:

- Describe the role of perseverance and determination in the success of entrepreneurs.
- Describe ways in which adversity can be an advantage.
- Compare personal challenges with those of the Ice House entrepreneurs.
- Discuss how practicing persistence can shape one's mindset.
- Understand how concepts from this lesson can support college success.

Chalkboard Notes, Part 1

_____
_____
_____
_____
_____
_____
_____
_____
_____
_____
_____
_____
_____
_____
_____
_____
_____
_____
_____
_____
_____
_____
_____
_____
_____
_____
_____
_____
_____

Student-Generated Discussion, Part 1

Once you have viewed this part of the Chalkboard Lesson, think about the core concepts contained in each lesson and create 1 or 2 questions or topics that you would like to discuss in class. Also, write a brief response to one of the following four prompts prior to the next in-class session.

1. Which concept from this Chalkboard Lesson was most intriguing to you? Why?
2. Which entrepreneur's comments most sparked your interest in this lesson? Why?
3. How do the concepts in this lesson apply to an entrepreneurial mindset?
4. How does this portion of Uncle Cleve's story resonate with your own life?

Submit your discussion questions and responses to your facilitator prior to the corresponding in-class session.

In-Class Discussion Notes, Part 1

Chalkboard Notes, Part 2

Student-Generated Discussion, Part 2

Once you have viewed this part of the Chalkboard Lesson, think about the core concepts contained in each lesson and create 1 or 2 questions or topics that you would like to discuss in class. Also, write a brief response to one of the following four prompts prior to the next in-class session.

1. Which concept from this Chalkboard Lesson was most intriguing to you? Why?
2. Which entrepreneur's comments most sparked your interest in this lesson? Why?
3. How do the concepts in this lesson apply to an entrepreneurial mindset?
4. How does this portion of Uncle Cleve's story resonate with your own life?

Submit your discussion questions and responses to your facilitator prior to the corresponding in-class session.

In-Class Discussion Notes, Part 2

Application Assignment

As you now know, the Opportunity Discovery Process is an iterative, experimental process that requires interaction and observation, as well as experimentation and adaptation. It is a process that can uncover unexpected obstacles, as well as unforeseen opportunities. For most, the secret to success is perseverance and determination.

Now that you understand the Opportunity Discovery Process, it is time to compare your own experience with that of a successful entrepreneur from your own community.

Group Assignment: For this assignment, your group will identify and interview a successful entrepreneur or small business owner. Your goal is to use the Opportunity Discovery Canvas to gain an understanding of his or her entrepreneurial journey so that you can compare and contrast it with your own.

Using the Opportunity Discovery Canvas as a guide, consider asking the following questions:

1. Why did you become an entrepreneur? What were the circumstances that led you to become an entrepreneur?
2. What was your original idea and where did it come from?
3. What problems were you trying to solve?
4. Who were your first customers and how did you convince them to buy? How did you find more customers to grow the business?
5. Did your idea catch on quickly or did it grow slowly over time?
6. Where did you get the money to get started?
7. What skills were most important in the early days of your journey?
8. What skills did you need to learn?
9. What unexpected challenges did you encounter?
10. What unexpected opportunities did you discover?

Group Directive: Take detailed notes during the interview. Once the interview is complete, fill in a separate Opportunity Discovery Canvas using details from your selected entrepreneur's story. Fill in the canvas as if you are documenting a snapshot of his or her Opportunity Discovery Process.

Back of the Canvas Analysis: Complete the Notes section on the backside of the canvas worksheet (approximately 100-150 words) by considering the following questions:

- Provide a brief description of the entrepreneur's journey.
- Compare and contrast it to your own.
- Which aspects of his or her story are similar?
- Which aspects are different?

Note: You should also begin to prepare for your final group presentation.

Ice House Opportunity Discovery Canvas

1. Describe the problem you want to solve.

2. Describe the type of people who have this problem.

3. How are they currently solving the problem?

PROBLEM

4. Describe your proposed solution.

5. How will your solution be different?

6. Will people pay for your solution?

SOLUTION

7. How will potential customers know about your solution?

8. How will potential customers purchase your solution?

9. Why will potential customers purchase your solution?

CONNECTION

NOTES

Provide a brief description of the entrepreneur's journey. Compare and contrast it with your own. What have you learned from this experience and how can it be applied to your own discovery process? Which of your assumptions were accurate and which of them have changed?

_____

_____

_____

_____

_____

_____

_____

_____

_____

_____

_____

_____

_____

_____

_____

_____

_____

_____

_____

_____

_____

_____

_____

_____

_____

_____

_____

_____

_____

_____

Application Assignment Rubric

Score / Criteria	3	2	1	0
QUANTITY & ACCOUNTABILITY Central questions and directives in the assignment are addressed	☐ A successful entrepreneur or small business person is interviewed by the group ☐ Opportunity Discovery Canvas is filled in documenting entrepreneur's own discovery process ☐ Notes section on the back side of the canvas worksheet is completed (approximately 100-150 words) ☐ Assignment is submitted on time	☐ A successful entrepreneur or small business person is interviewed by the group ☐ Opportunity Discovery Canvas is filled in documenting entrepreneur's own discovery process ☐ Notes section on the back side of the canvas worksheet is completed (approximately 100-150 words) ☐ Assignment is submitted on time	☐ Interview takes place Interview is documented on canvas Notes section on the back side of the canvas worksheet is completed	☐ Interview does not take place and/or canvas documentation is not submitted
QUALITY & CONNECTION Information sources are relevant, and assignment demonstrates critical thinking skills	☐ Person interviewed is a genuine entrepreneur (not manager, employee, volunteer, etc) ☐ Interview utilizes 10 suggested interview questions ☐ Team members all take detailed notes during interview and contribute to completing canvas ☐ Opportunity Discovery Canvas synthesizes interview notes into a coherent snapshot of entrepreneur's Opportunity Discovery Process. ☐ Notes on back of canvas compare and contrast entrepreneur's journey with your own	☐ Person interviewed is a genuine entrepreneur (not manager, employee, volunteer, etc) ☐ Interview questions are drawn from suggested question set ☐ Team members take notes and most contribute to completing canvas ☐ Opportunity Discovery Canvas is completely filled out using details from your selected entrepreneur's story. ☐ Notes on back of canvas compare and contrast entrepreneur's journey with your own	☐ Person interviewed is a genuine entrepreneur (not manager, employee, volunteer, etc) ☐ Interview question set is not followed or is incomplete ☐ It can be difficult to understand the entrepreneur's success story, because details are lacking, or match to canvas boxes is not obvious ☐ Notes section comparing entrepreneur's journey with your own is only sketched in, or parallels are not clearly drawn	☐ Interview does not take place and/or canvas documentation is not submitted

Peer Workshop Notes

Reflection Assignment

Reflection assignments are designed to encourage you to write reflectively about what you are learning and to explore ideas more deeply. These assignments also provide an opportunity to think about the future you want to create for yourself and how best to apply the knowledge you have gained in a way that will enable you to accomplish your goals.

Entrepreneurship is not about how to get rich quick and expecting it to be easy is a mistake. The so-called secret behind every entrepreneur's success is hard work, perseverance and determination.

Assignment: Reflect on the following questions:

1. Of the eight entrepreneurs featured in this lesson, which inspires you the most? Why?
2. What challenges did they entrepreneur overcome? How do these challenges compare to your own?
3. If knowledge and effort (rather than luck and circumstances) are the keys that empower entrepreneurs to succeed, what are you willing to give up in order to accomplish your goals?
4. What stands out to you, feels new to you, excites you, or challenges you from this lesson?

Your reflection should demonstrate evidence of in-depth reflective thinking. Your viewpoints and interpretations should be insightful and supported by clear examples.

Final Presentation

Assignment: Now that you are familiar with the Opportunity Discovery Process, it is time to present your ideas in a final presentation. This presentation will provide an opportunity to demonstrate the evolution of your ideas and learning throughout the Opportunity Discovery Process while receiving any final feedback from your peers.

For this final presentation, we also suggest that you invite expert mentors, advisors or other entrepreneurs that you may have interacted with to attend. Facilitators may choose to invite several expert mentors and entrepreneurs to participate on a panel to offer additional guidance and support.

Guidelines: Your presentation should be approximately 8-10 minutes long, and should expand upon the ideas and observations you shared in the midterm presentation. Engage your audience and be sure to demonstrate enthusiasm and professionalism while presenting. You may use a PowerPoint presentation, the Opportunity Discovery Canvas or other visual aids in your presentation. However it is important to remember that visual aids should complement, not replace face-to-face communication.

An additional 3-5 minutes should be set aside to respond to feedback and questions from your peers or expert mentors and advisors, who may also attend. We strongly suggest that you include all members of your group in the presentation. For more details on grading criteria for these presentations, consult the detailed presentation rubric.

Group Directive: Using the entire canvas as a guide, clearly and concisely address the following questions in your group presentation. Provide specific examples from your Opportunity Discovery Process:

1. What was your original idea?
2. How has your idea changed through the customer interviews from your out-of-the-building experience?
3. What else did you learn from academic and other out-of-the-building knowledge sources?
4. Will you proceed with your idea? If so, how will you expand your idea and connect with more customers? If not, why not?
5. What are your next action steps beyond this course? What opportunities will you pursue in your personal, academic and/or professional life?

When your presentation is complete, listen attentively to the other presentations and provide constructive feedback to your peers. After all, collaboration is key to developing new ideas and improving your problem-solution fit.

Final Presentation Rubric

Score / Criteria	3	2	1	0
QUANTITY & ACCOUNTABILITY Central questions and directives in the assignment are addressed	□ Presentation is 8 - 10 minutes long □ Facilitated question and answer follow up is 3 – 5 minutes long □ All members of the team participate in the presentation and demonstrate shared understanding of the group's canvas Process □ Content for presentation is drawn from entire canvas	□ Presentation is 8 - 10 minutes long □ Facilitated question and answer follow up is 3 – 5 minutes long □ All members of the team participate in the presentation and demonstrate shared understanding of the group's canvas Process □ Content for presentation is drawn from entire canvas	□ Presentation is less than 8 minutes long □ Question and answer follow up takes place □ Most members of the team participate in the presentation. Individual participation of all team members is uneven □ Content for presentation is drawn from entire canvas	□ Does not present
QUALITY & CONNECTION Content is derived from canvas search process, and assignment demonstrates critical thinking and presentation skills	□ Presentation demonstrates professionalism through evidence of design, logical flow, preparation and practice. □ Ideas are communicated clearly and concisely □ Team's enthusiasm engages audience □ Visual graphic aids enhance the speakers' message □ Presentation expands upon the ideas and observations shared at the midterm □ Changes in the idea are reported, and backed up with relevant supporting details from knowledge gained through Opportunity Discovery Process (customer interviews and other knowledge sources) □ Decision of whether or not to proceed with idea is communicated and justified □ Next action steps to proceed with idea or pursue opportunities in personal, academic, and/or professional life beyond course are outlined □ Questions and feedback are respectfully received and competently answered	□ Presentation demonstrates professionalism through evidence of design, preparation and practice. □ Team's enthusiasm engages audience □ Visual graphic aids enhance the speakers' message, rather than distracting from it □ Presentation expands upon the ideas and observations shared at the midterm □ Changes in the idea are reported, and follow directly from knowledge gained through Opportunity Discovery Process (customer interviews and other knowledge sources) □ Next action steps beyond course are outlined □ Questions and feedback are respectfully received and competently answered	□ Presentation is generally comprehensible, but may benefit from clearer organization □ Presentation delivery is informal, or efforts to purposefully engage audience are minimal □ Ideas may ramble or be underdeveloped □ Presentation may or may not expand on ideas and observations shared at midterm □ Changes in idea are reported, but clear explanatory links to knowledge gained through Opportunity Discovery Process may not be evident □ Decision whether or not to proceed with idea may not be communicated □ Next action steps may or may not be outlined □ Questions and feedback are respectfully received and answered	□ Does not present

Personal Vision Statement and Ice House Analysis

This assignment consists of two components that are designed to assess your knowledge and comprehension from the Ice House course, as well as your ability to apply this knowledge to your success as a student and in life.

Personal Vision Statement

You began this course by describing the future you want to create, as well as the greatest obstacles that stand in your way. Throughout the course, you had opportunities to reflect on the core concepts within each lesson and how they can be applied in a way that will enable you to overcome the obstacles necessary to accomplish your goals. Now, for this final assignment, reflect on what you have learned from the entire course and how it may have altered or influenced your vision for the future you want to create.

Assignment: Develop a 2-3 page vision statement that describes your vision of the future you want to create for yourself. This statement should also describe how you will apply the knowledge you have gained to overcome obstacles and accomplish your goals.

Consider responding to the following questions:

1. Now that you have completed this course, what is the future you envision for yourself?
2. How has your personal vision evolved since the beginning of the course?
3. What are the most important things you now want to make happen both as a student and in personal your life?
4. What skills do you now need to learn?
5. What are the greatest obstacles that might prevent you from accomplishing your goals?
6. How will you overcome these obstacles?
7. What do you need to start doing? What do you need to stop doing?
8. What do you need to do more of? What do you need to do less of?

Ice House Analysis

Now we will give you a chance to share what you learned from the Ice House Entrepreneurship Program, and express why taking this course was important to you. This part of the assignment should become an analysis of the journey you took throughout the course, as well as a road map for how you will accomplish your goals.

Assignment: In 2 to 3 pages, respond in depth to the following questions. Illustrate your thoughts using specific examples from the book, the chalkboard lessons and the Ice House entrepreneurs.

1. Which of the Ice House entrepreneurs inspired you most and why? (Choose at least 1)
   a. How has this entrepreneur affected your mindset or personal vision?
2. Which of the chalkboard lessons resonated with you most and why? (Choose at least 2)
   a. How have these lessons affected your mindset or personal vision?
3. What is the most important thing you have learned from the Ice House program?
4. How will what you learned from the Ice House course help you succeed in college?
5. How do ordinary people like Uncle Cleve, those with no particular advantage in life, manage to succeed regardless of their circumstances?

Personal Vision Statement Rubric

Score	3	2	1	0
Criteria				
QUANTITY & ACCOUNTABILITY Central questions and directives in the assignment are addressed	☐ Writes and submits Personal Vision Statement (2–3 pages) ☐ Writes and submits Ice House Analysis essay (2-3 pages) ☐ Assignments are submitted on time	☐ Writes and submits Personal Vision Statement (2–3 pages) ☐ Writes and submits Ice House Analysis essay (2-3 pages) ☐ Assignments are submitted on time	☐ Writes and submits Personal Vision Statement (1–2 pages) ☐ Writes and submits Ice House Analysis essay (1-2 pages)	☐ Does not submit Vision Statement and Ice House Analysis
QUALITY & CONNECTION Content is derived from canvas search process, and assignment demonstrates critical thinking and presentation skills	☐ Personal Vision Statement describes the future student wants to create for self ☐ Personal Vision Statement describes how knowledge gained from the course will be applied to overcome obstacles and accomplish personal, academic, and professional goals ☐ Ice House Analysis analyzes impact of Ice House course on own journey, including description of a road map forward ☐ Thoughts are illustrated and clear connections made using specific examples from: the book, at least 2 Chalkboard lessons, and more than one Ice House entrepreneur. ☐ Writing is high quality- with well-organized structure, proper sentences, and almost no grammar mistakes	☐ Personal Vision Statement describes the future student wants to create for self ☐ Personal Vision Statement discusses how knowledge gained from course will be applied to overcome obstacles and accomplish goals ☐ Ice House Analysis describes impact of Ice House course on own journey ☐ Thoughts are illustrated and clear connections are made with specific examples from: the book, at least 2 Chalkboard lessons, and at least one Ice House entrepreneur. ☐ Writing is decent- with organized structure and a few grammar mistakes	☐ Personal Vision Statement describes the future student wants to create for self ☐ Personal Vision Statement cites knowledge gained from the course, but may not directly apply it to a personal plan to overcome obstacles and accomplish goals ☐ Most personally important lesson learned from Ice House program is stated. ☐ Thoughts are illustrated using examples from: the book, Chalkboard lessons, and/or Ice House entrepreneurs. ☐ Writing is mediocre- with sloppy paragraph structure, disorganized sentences and several grammar mistakes.	☐ Does not submit Vision Statement and Ice House Analysis